CONVERSATIONS

WITH

Milton H. Erickson, M.D.

VOLUME 3

Changing Children
and Families

John Weakland   Gregory Bateson   Jay Haley
Palo Alto, California — 1950's

CONVERSATIONS
WITH
Milton H. Erickson, M.D.

VOLUME 3

Changing Children
and Families

Edited by

Jay Haley

 TRIANGLE PRESS

Library of Congress Catalog Card Number 84-052027

ISBN 0-931513-03-0

Published by Triangle Press
Distributed by W. W. Norton & Co., Inc., 500 Fifth Avenue,
  New York, N. Y. 10110
W. W. Norton & Co., Ltd., 37 Great Russell Street, London,
  WC1B3NU

CONTENTS

INTRODUCTION

This volume contains conversations with Milton H. Erickson about his ways of dealing with whole families and his therapy of children. In Volumes 1 and 2 of this series are presented his conversations about changing individuals and changing marital couples. Included as an appendix in this volume is a conversation with him about his life which provides biographical information not published before.

The reader unfamiliar with Dr. Erickson will find in these conversations a lively presentation of his ideas and approach to therapy. The reader who has read everything written about Erickson will find new material as well as the basic data of his views expressed in his own words. Some of the case reports will be familiar because I drew upon these conversations for my book, *Uncommon Therapy*.* A few cases Erickson told to other people who have since published them. The Erickson scholar will have the opportunity to examine these transcripts of what Erickson actually said and compare them with the summaries of authors who have written about his work.

The conversations in this particular volume took place from 1958 to 1961 and were part of Gregory Bateson's research project investigation of family therapy, an adventure we had just begun at that time. For several years the project had been studying Erickson's hypnosis and therapy as part of a larger investigation of the nature of therapeutic change. Besides our research interest, John Weak-

---

*Haley, J. *Uncommon Therapy*, New York, Norton, 1973.

land and I were doing therapy in private practice and so had a practical concern for learning how therapy should be done. Bateson participated in these conversations with both a research interest and a wish to have guidance with a family he was doing therapy with as part of the project.

The first conversations in this volume about therapy with whole families took place in 1958. The reader should keep in mind that we questioners were just beginners in dealing with families in that early time. We had done our first interview with a whole family in 1956, and by April 1957 I was interviewing a family and we called it family therapy. At that time there were, at most, one or two people anywhere, that we knew about, interviewing whole families. Dr. Erickson was one of the people who did therapy with families, as we had learned when talking with him about other matters beginning in 1955. Therefore, we sought him out to gather information about his therapy approach for research reasons and also to consult with him about the therapy we were attempting with families. We had no one else with experience to consult.

I say all this because I wish to emphasize that the views we project members expressed about families at that time were comments by beginners; they are not an expression of the views we would hold today. In fact, I am embarrassed by some of the comments and questions. They are often the kind of comments which irritate me with trainees today. We were rather negative, pessimistic, often anti-parent and anti-mother. More important, we were confusing our research descriptions with ideas needed to do therapy. A communication description of a family was not necessarily helpful if one set out to change a family, and we were just learning that theory for research and theory for change are not the same. In defense, it might be noted that we had been doing this kind of therapy hardly more than a year, and we were working with the most difficult types of families – those families with a hospitalized member diagnosed as schizophrenic.

As I read these conversations now, its seems evident that Dr. Erickson was often both puzzled and patient with us. When we gave a complex, negative description of a family, he would respond with an inquiry about our therapy goal and how what we were saying was relevant to what we were trying to do. His emphasis was on operations to induce a change, while we were concerned with a research description, if not a philosophical one, about the family.

These conversations are presented to bring out Erickson's views about dealing with families, not to present those of the questioners. My views today are different, both about family therapy in general and about techniques with families containing a schizophrenic in particular. It seems now that the sensible goal is to help the problem young person function normally and the family organize to make that happen. That is the view Dr. Erickson had at that time. When we were emphasizing discussing with the family their communication process, he was emphasizing that one should help the young person and family disengage and have a normal life. That is what sensible therapists do today, and the reader might keep in mind that getting to that point took experience and trial and error with a variety of difficult families. Erickson had taken some of those steps previous to these conversations.

The recordings of these conversations were not made to present Erickson's ideas to the world but as a way of taking notes for research purposes. Therefore, the reader will not find the conversations systematic and complete but often scattered with a number of interruptions. Sometimes these interruptions are practical ones, such as for telephone calls or breaks during the day. At other times they are indications of a break in the conversation for a period of time. The arrangement here is largely by year, beginning with the earliest one and progressing forward.

For the research-minded, the recordings of these conversations are on file with the Erickson Foundation in Phoenix, Arizona.

CHAPTER 1

Family Interview
Technique and the
Trauma That Cures

1958. Present were Milton H. Erickson, Gregory Bateson, Jay Haley, and John Weakland.

Bateson: We want to talk to you about your experiences in working with husbands and wives, husbands and wives and children. How one deals with multiple patient situations. How *you* deal with multiple patient situations. And about the dynamics of families that have schizophrenics in them.

Erickson: You want a discussion from me, unformulated, as to how I would approach the situation with a given family.

B: There are various ways this can be done. We can run you (audio)tapes of families, or John and Jay have specific questions. I have some myself.

E: Why don't you conduct it the way you think it should be conducted.

B: Well, let's start the way John thought it should be conducted, by asking you questions rather than throwing data at you. It is your data in the back of your head that we are after.

1

Weakland: My idea of the way to conduct things is that it would be profitable to start more or less the way Jay and I have worked at getting information from you before in the course of our several visits to Phoenix. We have certain questions about families and dealing with them, and we ought to try and bring some of those up first.

E: Well, there is something I think that I ought to say first. If I'm going to interview a father and mother and son, or a father, mother and daughter, or two children, to begin that interview, to preface it, to lay the foundation, I happen to mention that father is sitting in *that* chair. Of course mother is sitting in that other chair, and sister is sitting over here, and brother is sitting over here. I make mention of that in several ways so that I define them geographically. That way I give each one of them a position, a spatial position in the interview. By giving them this spatial position in the interview, when I talk to them, I talk to that particular space, and the others listen in. When that person talks to me, the others listen in. So I get that spatial compartmentalization. That considerably prevents the others from barging in, and forces the others unwittingly to take an objective view, at least in part. It's a rather simple procedure. That's all I have to say on that.

W: Well, I take it that when you deal with families, at times you see them all together, and at times you will separate out one or two members and talk to them separately. So that you work both ways.

E: I work both ways. I may interview the family jointly, and then I'll put one member out. But after I send the other members out, I again redefine the position in which those members were. I usually give the wife a certain chair, and then the husband this chair over here, and the children, or the child, the chairs in between. Then if I send mother and child out of the room, I'll carefully move father from his chair into mother's chair. Quite often I'll have mother, when she comes back, sit in child's chair, or in husband's chair, at least temporarily.

W: So that you define the position, but you indicate that they can sit in somebody else's seat, so to speak, for a while.

E: That's right. "As you sit where your son sat, maybe you can think more clearly about him through that association." "If you sit where your husband sat, maybe it will give you somewhat of his view of me as I sit here." Thus I force them into an objective role about their organization. I tell the child, "Well, suppose you sit in mother's seat." "Suppose you sit in father's seat." Also, from time to time when I repeat the interviews with the entire family, I shuffle them about so that while mother had this chair originally, for the next two or three interviews, all of a sudden, the family grouping is rearranged. Yet it's a family grouping, but mother's chair has now become the one that used to be father's chair. I can think of the family that I saw just recently: father's chair, mother's chair, big sister's chair, younger sister's chair. I maneuvered that around because not one of them would talk and tell me the situation. So I maneuvered their positions. When younger sister got into big sister's chair, younger sister gave me an awful lot of information. Father couldn't talk to me in *his* chair. His statement was, "My mind just goes blank." But in mother's chair he gave a lot of information. I carefully defined their positions because I wanted to start to handle that situation. I knew it was going to be critical.

Haley: Do you have general rules on when you send the family out and talk to one member alone, or why you don't consistently deal with them all at the same time?

E: I watch the interplay between inhibitions, hesitation, antagonism, resentment — something of that sort. Anything that indicates that they could think about it differently but not as long as the other person is there. Or if I see any evidence of a separate set of ideas that they are withholding. Then I know that I've got to deal with them separately.

W: Then you'd have to do something later about bringing that separate set of ideas in.

E: After I've gotten the information, then I interview the group, and I can point out that necessarily mother, being a woman, really has different views about what's going on in the family. Because father's working during the day, and he sees the family only when he's tired at night. And one gets more "iffy" with fatigue. In that way I justify . . .

W: You sort of legitimize differences in view when they come back in.

E: So that they can come back in and they hear me legitimize their differences.

W: I know that the family I work with tends to swing back and forth, at least on the parental part. The son is the sick one, ostensibly; the boy is in the hospital. The parents swing back and forth between insisting that they don't have any differences and insisting that they have practically nothing but differences, with a clear implication that they have different views and things are impossible. So I find myself grappling repeatedly with this in trying to get across the idea that differences in view do exist, but they don't mean that life is impossible.

E: Jay Haley has spoken about my tendency to use analogies. When people start disagreeing in that fashion I like to offer an analogy. When they try to tell me that they are in disagreement and they must think in common, I point out to them, "Yes, father likes meat rare, and mother likes it well done, and sister likes it medium. And they all eat the same meal." Any kind of an analogy that allows them to agree with you that there is a common thread. I don't care how good that analogy is, but I mention it.

B: Tweedle dum and tweedle dee agreed to have a battle.

E: Yes. Why shouldn't they agree to battle? Why shouldn't they agree to disagree? I bring that out when dealing with father and mother. When she says, "I disagree with you," I ask father, "Do you really understand your wife? Your wife says that she disagrees with you. That means that she has a totally different opinion. And you agree that she has a totally different opinion. (Laughter) Because I'd like to have that clearly understood, that she does have a different opinion. That means you are in agreement with her, and you can agree with her being different from you, and she can agree with you that your feeling is different from hers." Then I've got an agreement.

H: Milton, how do you deal with a couple or a family busy proving to you that he or she is the one in the right? They tend to pull the therapist in and prove to the therapist they're right, and they get into competition proving who's innocent.

E: They prove that they are right, and the other person is wrong. They want to pull you in on their side, and I keep out of that situation by saying to father, "You and I are going to listen. Your wife is going to point out to *you*, and to *me*, the matter in which she is right and justified, and *we* are going to listen." You see, I shift from *you* and *I* to *we*, but I am allying *him* with *me*.

H: At the moment the mother is trying to ally you with her.

E: At the very moment the mother is trying to ally me with her, I deliberately ally myself with father and *we* are going to listen sympathetically and intelligently to mother. Then mother has to present her case to father and to me because we are listening intelligently. Now mother knows that father can't listen intelligently, but she knows *I* can. That's why she's talking to me, but father and I are listening; *we* are listening intelligently. She has to credit father with listening intelligently. So I've got her over there talking to *we*, and then I can turn to mother and say, "Now you have explained this, and *we* have been trying to understand the best way we can. Now suppose you and I listen to father's understanding of what you said, and as we listen we can recognize how well he understands it. And we ought to know every one of his good understandings. We really ought to." So my alliance has suddenly switched to mother. She and I are allied while father is explaining.

W: This also sort of keeps a balance, rather than letting one person get hold of everything in a situation. That is, if mother has the floor to present her views, father has the alliance, and then the other way around, so that no person gets the whole advantage at one time.

E: I am the hub.

W: Around which it all revolves.

E: Yes. In that way I can play almost a passive part, and yet each has to rely upon me. They can't rely on me without giving credit to the other person. You do the same thing for the child in the total situation. Johnny and father and I will listen, and as *we* listen, mother presents.

W: What about the matter of the child speaking up? I wonder if this presents any differences.

E: Oh yes.

W: It's sort of presented as having differences, and there are some real differences.

E: It's a very real difference, and therefore, with father and mother present, I ally myself openly with the child.

"Now you and I are going to listen. First to your mother, and next to your father. And we can think about what they're saying, and we can know what's *wrong* in what they say." With father and mother the emphasis is on recognizing what is *right*. With the child the emphasis is on knowing what is wrong in what father and mother are saying.

H: Why that difference?

E: Because you see the child knows his parents are wrong. The child belongs to another generation. The child has a different background of understanding. And you convey to the parents that the child thinks they are wrong. You're merely using what they already know. It is an error to try to tell the child that his parents are right, when he knows they are wrong. That's the child's orientation. The parents *are* in error, and the parents know that the child *thinks* they are wrong. But a couple of adults think that they ought to be right; that's a general assumption. "You're a full-grown person, you really ought to think right, you ought to understand right." "No, you're a child, you don't understand, you're wrong, you're mistaken." The child thinks, "Yes, just because you're a grownup, you aren't right." You see it's a totally different point of view.

W: I understand that, in part, you're picking up the fact that the parents are drawing such a big line between themselves as adults, and the child as a child, that you go along with that and turn it around.

E: I turn it around.

H: And you continue this even though the child is reasonably adult, say in the teens?

E: In the teens. Why certainly.

B: Especially in the teens.

E: Because the teenager so thoroughly knows his parents are wrong.

W: What about the matter of the child speaking out as well as listening to what is wrong in what his parents are saying? Do you encourage the kids to point out the way they see things?

E: Sometimes I point out, by asking the child, "Now suppose you and I sit very quietly, and let us note in what way mother is wrong, and then we'll listen to father and note in what way he's wrong." Then we ask mother to explain the situation, and then we ask father to explain the situation. And we note particularly in what way they are both wrong on the same things, which then allows the child to recognize mother is wrong on certain things in a different way than father is wrong on certain things, but they're both wrong in certain ways. Then I can ask the child who's listening, "Your mother won't believe it, but you can actually point out *some* things where she's mistaken, she's really wrong. The same thing holds true for father. You can actually point out *some* things where father is wrong, but he won't believe it." But you know mother will believe it on these particular things. Just as father will believe it on certain things in relationship to mother. Because they're wrong in different ways on some things. But they aren't going to believe it when they're both wrong on the same thing in the same way. Then the child starts thinking about where mother is wrong in her special way, where the father and child and I will agree but mother won't. Then the child is free to verbalize on that.

W: He has to be given some room to maneuver in.

E: To maneuver, and he's got allies. Mother is wrong in this special way, father and I are allied, so the child is in a good situation to verbalize. You switch the child over, and mother is allied with me, and he points out that special way in which mother can recognize that father is wrong. And you've got an awful lot of action there.

H: The way you present it, Milton, they're just responding so nicely; this will give you this, will give you this, will give you this. Now when you are actually in there mixing with a family, they're all going at once, or if they're not all going at once, the feeling gets so strong that they don't respond in this quiet way that you are presenting. Now how do you keep them, other than spatial orientation, speaking when *you* want them to speak, and allying with you in a way that *you* want them to ally?

E: That's where I get authoritative. If I think there's any possibility of them talking all at once, I tell them, "Now just pause, just listen to me briefly. I'm going to say certain things, and then I'm going to have you talk, and then brother, and then sister, and then mother, and I want you to do one of two things, either you listen when the other is talking, or turn your back and note in what way they are wrong. You'll have to be silent as you do that, in order to note in what way they are wrong." And I demonstrate to them how to turn their back to their seat, and then when they just can't contain themselves, I say, "Now turn your backs a little bit more." (Laughter)

H: Give them something to do.

E: Give them something to do that expresses their attitude, their feeling, just as competently as verbalization. You watch a wife turn her back to the husband and listen. And she's got her *back* turned toward him.

W: This begins to make it clear-cut, you know, instead of having it with our families where they're doing two things at once all mixed together.

E: But you see that turning of back is very expressive. Then I can tell the husband, if he can't take that sort of interference, "All right, keep on with your explanation. Your wife's really got her back turned toward you emphatically. I'm approving of your wife's nonverbal participation. So that you can tell it to me

better, suppose you just turn your back to her." So
I've got him in competition with his wife, back to
back, instead of voice to voice. So they've got their
interplay, but it's a silent, non-interfering interplay.

H: They can outshout each other with body movement.

E: Outshout each other with body movement. Each explains. Each will listen and take note of where the other
is wrong. If they had any intellectual background, I
can suggest that they note in an orderly fashion how
the other is wrong. Because when you note in orderly fashion, then you note in an intelligently critical
fashion. "Note in an orderly fashion." The people with
the college background, or highly intelligent people;
it's one way of getting them to be objectively critical.

H: Well, that's a way of handling it when they're angry and
anxious to talk. What about the reverse when they're
busy not talking because they're protecting each other,
and they are concerned about hurting each other's
feelings?

E: Well, then you build a situation up somewhat differently. That's less likely to occur, but you first build it up
in this way: "You know, if this interview is to be satisfactory, you have got to say a number of things that
won't be understood until after you have explained
them. So you will say something that in the first
sentence sounds unpleasant, or critical, or adverse
that might actually be painful, but as you add the
second sentence, the meaning of the first sentence
changes. Then as you add the third sentence, your
point will get clearer, and by the fourth . . . so I'm going to ask you to listen first to the first sentence, and
wait for the fourth and fifth sentence so that you will
be sure to understand the point that's being made. Remember this is an unrehearsed situation, and you
haven't had an opportunity to organize your thoughts,
and you're going to be just a little bit clumsy in the

way you say things, because you don't know just how to say these important things. Just as I am going to be clumsy at saying some of these things. Because I don't know what you are going to say. You won't always understand me the first time I say something. You won't always understand me the second. Many times I say it 4, 5, 6, 8, 10 times before *my* meaning gets clear."

Then if I think that they are too sensitive, I'll say, "Of course, you know, in order to clarify a difference of opinion we've got to have our feelings hurt. You've got to hurt my feelings by impressing upon me the thought that I can't understand a simple declaration on your part. You'll have to repeat it a half dozen times before it will get through to me." That implies that I'm not very bright; of course, I am not very bright in this situation. The same things are going to hold true for the wife. "You know as your wife explains things to me about you, your feelings are going to get hurt because she won't get through to you because she has to talk from a feminine point of view. You can talk from a masculine point of view. The two of you must talk from a marital point of view. I have to talk from a psychotherapy point of view." In that way I've defined certain geographical situations: psychotherapeutic, the masculine, the feminine, and the marital, which is separate from that. Then I add to them the family point of view. That is separate from the marital. I know that those are all more or less false categorizations, but the patients are concerned with them.

H: You define their hurt feelings as a misunderstanding, or a lack of understanding?

E: As a lack of understanding.

W: Which will be taken care of as things go on.

E: That's right. And an expectable and a warranted hurt feeling because certainly you can't expect all of it all at once in the first sentence. Then I can offer them an analogy that they can accept. "The child is awfully afraid of the hypodermic needle and is going to faint or scream or go into a panic when he feels the needle penetrating his skin. Don't you think you really ought to take ahold of that child and pinch his skin just a little and hurt him? Then you plunge the needle in. Because he's paying attention to that little bit of a pinch you're giving him, he doesn't notice the needle. And the child has got the medicine he needs. He's just wondering about why did you pinch me on the wrist?"

B: Is this what you say to them or your philosophy?

E: Well it's an analogy that I can give them. It's one that I've used about hurt feelings. To bring it out and to get the initial hurt feelings, to get something from an individual subsequently. Of course it is a good technique with children.

H: Well, there's more in that analogy than meets the eye when you're telling that to a couple about their feelings.

B: Mm hmm. (Laughs) They're busy needling each other.

E: Well, of course the thing that's in that analogy is the fact that you are stating very definitely that you are deliberately pinching. That there is a deliberate pinching. It's intentional, and it's for the purpose of hurting. It is essential to the situation, but it's preliminary to therapy. Then if they want to find fault with it, you ask them how they're going to distract the child's attention? Then they can't think of another way that's going to be successful, so they acknowledge that they are going to pinch.

*   *   *

E: I don't think I've given you this instance. There was a 14-year-old girl, rather stockily built, whose mother came to me because Ann had developed the idea, about three months previously, that her feet were much too large. Her mother thought it was that she thought her hips were too large, but the girl was most insistent that her *feet* were too large. So the girl had been very much of a problem. She didn't want to go to school or to be seen on the street. She wouldn't go to church. Her feet were too large. She was utterly adamant in her attitude about that. She was getting more and more seclusive, and mother consulted me because she couldn't get the daughter to go to a doctor. The daughter would not allow the subject of her feet to be discussed. Mother asked me if I could do something about it. So I arranged with mother that I would come over on the false pretense that I would do a chest examination of the mother to see if the mother really did have the flu. Since it would be Saturday, the girl would be at home. The mother wanted to know what I was going to do, but I had worked out my own plan. I knew the girl by sight. The girl called me, and when I got over there, the mother was in bed. I asked the girl to bring me a towel, and I asked her to stand right here, in case I wanted something else. I did a rather careful examination of the mother, and I sent the girl for a teaspoon so I could look at mother's throat, and then I had the girl hold a flashlight as I was looking at mother's eyes and mother's throat. In getting the girl to do things, I asked her to wait so that she could stand right there in case I needed her again. Finally I finished my examination, and I had maneuvered the girl into position. Then, before getting up, because I was sitting on the edge of the bed, I asked the girl just to wait; I thought I might have something else for her to do, just wait. And then I very slowly, and carefully, and thoughtfully, got up from the bed, talking to the mother, and then with the greatest of care I stepped back awkwardly, and very carefully stomped my heel squarely down on the girl's toes. The girl, of course, squawked with pain. I turned on her, and in a tone of absolute fury, I said to her, "If you would grow those things *large* enough for a *man* to see, I wouldn't be in this sort of a situation." The girl looked at me so puzzled. Before I had finished writing my prescription and calling it in to the drugstore, the girl asked her mother if she could go to a show. There was no further trouble. You see, the girl thought her feet were too large, and in the most beautifully convincing way, I had forced upon her a compliment. If she would grow her feet *large* enough for a man to see. There was no way of rejecting that compliment. There was no way of disputing. I certainly hadn't been trying to make her feel better. There was nothing for the girl to do but accept the absolute proof that her feet were small. There's no other way.

H: She had no more difficulty with her feet after that?

E: You see, I think it was a superficial manifestation, but the girl was caught in it. She was caught with her rationalization, and she was becoming more and more seclusive to substantiate her neurotic feeling, and she was building it up more and more. All I did was step right in with one forceful step and smashed the whole thing. What could she do about it? There was no answer. The girl couldn't tell me that I was clumsy, I was her mother's doctor. She couldn't retaliate in any way.

H: Did you see her again after that?

E: Oh yes. Friendly, agreeable, went to school, went to Sunday school, went to shows, that was the end of all of that three-month pattern of seclusiveness. And you see, when you consider a lot of neurotic manifestations, some little traumatic thing will precipitate progressively larger and larger neurosis. Why can't you take the same attitude toward the correction of neurosis? Take something that is in essence a traumatic thing, correctly orient it, and just thrust it upon the person in such a fashion that they have to accept it, and deal with it, and incorporate it.

H: The therapeutic trauma?

E: The therapeutic trauma.

B: Now the remarkable thing, which I don't understand, Milton, is, granted that episode and others like it, this must mean that in daily life we are all encountering such things with enormous frequency, really.

E: That's right.

B: Probably at the order of once or twice a day, certainly very high frequencies, and in daily life they are, in general, not carefully tailored to suit our needs, and why aren't we all nuts? (Laughs)

E: I know, we have to wait for something that appeals to us in particular.

B: The damaging thing would have to be as accurately tailored as the therapeutic?

E: Yes, and there are so many thousands of them. Among those thousands and thousands there's one that's tailored to fit. Just as I tailored that to fit Ann, and of course, you see, I had her in an anxiety situation. An anxiety situation in relationship to her mother. Was her mother really suffering serious illness? Having the girl assist me, holding the towel, and get another towel, and get a flashlight. The girl was anxious, and I built that up carefully. My listening to the chest, my percussion of the chest, my relistening, my entire demeanor, and the girl was very much attached to her mother.

H: Well, what does anxiety contribute to the situation?

E: The girl was withdrawing from society because of her anxiety about her feet. So let's have an anxious situation in which to trample on her feet. And have a complete setting there. So there's the anxiety situation into which her feet came, and then the utterance which the girl was forced to accept in all of its implications.

B: How do you know that the mother is not going to tip her hand?

E: I don't.

B: You're keeping her in line all the way down the line?

E: Yes, but you see mother couldn't know.

B: Mother knows the medical examination is phony.

E: Yes, but you see I also pointed out to mother that while the medical examination was a phony, one never knows when you *do* pick up things.

H: You assume the possibility of mother ending this, or frustrating this?

E: Oh yes. But you see the mother didn't know what I was going to do about Ann. She certainly couldn't see through that situation. All she could notice was that I certainly was impolite to her. The next thing she would discover was that Ann wanted to go to a show. And that would confront her with another insoluble thing, and she wouldn't be able to understand that.

H: She couldn't defeat you because she couldn't connect the two?

E: She wouldn't be able to connect the two in a way that would defeat me.

W: Would you say that the mother was also the sort of woman on whom your statement, "And you never know what you might have picked up," would hit her rather strongly? I just sort of wondered if somehow she might have also been a woman who was rather anxious about her own health or anxious about things in general.

E: Well, she was a bit anxious, and the examination relieved the mother's anxiety. Of course, Ann would see mother's anxiety, and she would see it relieved, because I examined the heart, I examined the breasts, I examined the lungs, I examined the throat, and the eyes.

W: So that your procedure was rather tailored to the mother as well as to the girl.

E: Tailored to the mother. Tailored to the total situation. I was very careful to palpate the thyroid, feel for tenderness in the mastoid area, I felt of her scalp. So that mother and the girl could see it was a very complete and adequate examination. Of course, during it I questioned the mother about the frequency of colds.

W: How old was this gal?

E: She was 14, and she had been maturing physically rather rapidly.

W: I was wondering about that.

E: Yes. With that rapid physical maturing and that psychological withdrawing, you could have a very pathological pattern built up.

W: You get a situation in which she would start to go back just when she should be coming out.

E: Yes.

B: On a point of fact, the mother comes to you without the girl, you have not seen the girl?

E: Oh, I had seen her casually. Because on one occasion I had seen her father, and I'd seen the girl, but not as a person.

B: One of the things that always mystifies me about these carefully tailored operations is how you know enough about that girl to be able to tailor. I mean you hadn't really; you had seen her casually at best.

E: Yes. You see while I was examining the chest and the girl brought me the towel, and then held the flashlight, and then brought me a spoon, I had no tailored plan in mind.

B: Oh it isn't tailored till toward the end of this medical examination then?

E: Till the end. I was wondering how I could present something to the girl, and that's why I asked the girl a number of questions. Because I could ask the mother how often she had colds, and then I could ask Ann, "Is your mother about right in her statements about how often she has colds?" You see, just to get the girl in a situation so I would have some kind of chance to clinically evaluate the girl. Then as soon as I felt that perhaps I had some understanding, the idea came to me, and I maneuvered her into place. You see, the entire thing that concerned me was how can I convey to this girl that her feet are not hideously large? How can I get her to accept that idea? How can I force it upon her without seeming to force it upon her?

H: It's a difficult problem all right, because any mention of her feet would have meant that you noticed her feet.

E: That's right. You take the girl who is very, very fat and is convinced that she is horribly, horribly unattractive. There's no way of telling her that she's attractive except in a traumatic fashion. I can think of Judy, and Judy knew that she was much too fat. Judy was horribly fat. She would go to church regularly, and she was a very prudent and prudish girl. She came to me as a patient about this matter of reducing, and she cheerfully told me how horribly unattractive she was. I'd seen her sitting outside of the office, and I could see the sort of behavior she was exhibiting. So when she came in, after I had her sit down and was courteous about it, I took that paperweight and asked her to tell me the story. I listened to her and what she had to say, looking at the paperweight and glancing at her. I kept right on just giving these brief glances at her. I got her entire story while I directed most of my visual attention to the paperweight. When she had finished, she wondered if I would be willing to accept her as a patient considering that she was so hideously unattractive. She said even if she did reduce, she would still be about the ugliest girl in creation. My statement was rather simply this, "I hope you'll forgive me for what I have done. I haven't faced you. I know it's rude. I've played with this paperweight, it's been rather difficult to look at you. I'd rather not tell you, but since this is a psychotherapeutic situation, I really ought to tell you. Perhaps you can find the explanation. But actually I have the very strong feeling that when you get reduced, at least everything I see about you, that's why I keep avoiding looking at you, indicates that when you get reduced you will be even more sexually attractive, which is something that should not be discussed between you and me. But you are, of course, extremely attractive sexually. You'll be much more so after you're reduced. But I think we ought not to discuss that matter here now." The first time the girl knew she was sexually attractive. I had proved it by my playing with that paperweight. All my argument was fallacious.

H: Then you can turn and give your full attention to her after just listening; this is something you won't talk about then.

E: Yes.

H: And that's traumatic to her?

E: The way she flushed, and the way she blushed, and the way she squirmed. I don't think it was too traumatic. (Laughter) But, of course, according to her codes, it was horribly unpleasant. According to her codes. But there was a man whom she respected immensely, who said that she was attractive sexually and would be even more so after she reduced. And who had noticed that sexual attractiveness immediately. But you see that play; I could have done it even if I hadn't recognized her feelings, because I like to keep myself free so that I can observe and then manipulate the situation. As soon as she started telling her story I saw her sense of physical inferiority and unattractiveness. Later she reduced and said she had fallen in love with an older man who was not interested in her. She let me know that she had fallen in love with an older man. A man almost old enough to be her father.

B: Did he play with paperweights?

E: He didn't play with paperweights, but he wouldn't play with her either. After she told me about that, I told her it was awfully nice she'd fallen in love with him. Very, very complimentary to him. Then, since she had learned to compliment a man, she would undoubtedly turn her affections to some man closer to her age. But she ought to keep on complimenting that older man for a while longer. That was a nice, easy, gradual loss of interest in him.

H: So simple, isn't it.

E: How do people develop their neurotic problems, and their neurotic feelings and attitudes? Very, very blindly, and yet nevertheless very elaborately. So why not assume that same blindness and that same elaborateness in the correction of them? Once you give them a push in the right direction. You know Judy couldn't turn down that compliment. Just as Ann couldn't turn down the compliment on her feet.

B: Well now, we would, in one of those cases, tend to assume—the girl with the feet—that the thing she's working out with her feet is related to things that mother and father, etc., are doing, and are interpersonal defenses to some degree. Therefore, to deprive her of that device would leave her open to some sort of attack from them of some kind. Now this might not be so; we might not think that in this case.

E: Yes, but why assume it must necessarily be an attack? There will also be support. She's open to both attack and to support, and there's a 50/50 chance. And you wait . . .

B: We see the patient remit during the week, go home for the weekend, and come back nuts.

W: Maybe there's a better choice of material. Let's see where the other 50 is.

E: Yes, but isn't that the tendency of psychotherapy? To see *only* the negative aspects?

W: Well, that's true. That's important.

E: And in Judy's case, I couldn't tell her that men see fat dames as attractive. I couldn't tell her that men see skinny dames as attractive. I couldn't tell her anything about sex appeal. She couldn't tolerate that. But I could explain my behavior. It was *my* behavior I was explaining. My avoidance behavior was explained. And she had seen it. I had apologized for it, and she had to accept *my* explanation. She had to recognize I had avoided looking at her. And that validated my statement she had sex appeal. Never mind the logic of it. (Laughter)

H: Well, presumably, when you were not looking at her, she was thinking that she was too unattractive for you to look at.

E: That's right. And she was wishing that she weren't that unattractive. That's the positive aspect.

H: Yes.

E: And my apology proved that there *was* that wishful aspect. My statement, "We should not discuss that," also validated her wishful thinking.

CHAPTER 2

Disengaging
Family Members

1958. Present were Milton H. Erickson, Jay Haley, and John Weakland.

H: Well, we're at the moment taking a look at the families of schizophrenics, trying to describe what goes on in these families, and ultimately trying to devise more practical methods of changing them. Actually we're in the process of therapy with them already, when we don't even know what we're after, we haven't described them, and we're not sure what changes we want, or what's crucial, and so on.

W: Really our thoughts come out of two things, I think: They come out of trying to deal with family groups, that is, father, mother and at least the schizophrenic patient. Sometimes we have a sibling in also. They come a little also out of some related questions from your practice where you're dealing with family problems of a different sort. But still, what we're concerned about is situations where you're dealing with more than one related person at a time. The focus is on the families of schizophrenics, but not exclusively.

H: Let's pose it this way. Suppose sitting here instead of us was a father who tended to find it difficult to agree or disagree with wife. And a mother who can be described in two ways: One, she has this unfortunate transfer of blame defense where it's always somebody else; the other that everything she says she qualifies in a contradictory way. When she's nice to you, she's nice in a mean way and mean in a nice way. And a patient, son or daughter—whenever this patient makes an assertive effort of any kind with regard to the parents, he or she takes it back or negates it. You have these three people and they're going round and round and round. Now what is your goal as far as relating to each of them?

E: How old is the child of the family?

H: Well let's say 21 or 22; schizophrenic.

E: I have such a family with children ages 23, 19, 17, and you've described the father *and* the mother. The therapy has been centered around first getting the older boy out of the home. Second, getting the second boy on his own. Third, getting the 17-year-old to move in with his 23-year-old, single brother and go to school.

H: Separation as rapidly as possible?

E: That's right. The father has never been allowed to have any of his own beliefs except by virtue of his dogged persistence. That is, he's an artist, but his wife has never allowed him to paint the pictures he's wanted to paint. So then he started working on ceramics. He made absolutely beautiful bowls and put on those bowls and cups and vases the pictures that he wanted to. Line drawings. Utterly beautiful. Until his wife suddenly discovered that he was having satisfaction there. He sneaked over to canvases, and to still life, and then to landscapes, then to portraits, then to historical scenes. Right at the present time he's sneaked over to sculpturing, but always remaining in the home and always coming to grief by virtue of his wife jumping on him.

H: While encouraging him, no doubt.

E: While encouraging him. "No John, you *must* do this."
Now with the older son moved out and in college, the
third son living with that son, and the second son
working and his own master completely, father is a
bit worried about mother because father has got a
summer artist teaching job away from home and he's
moving out. That leaves poor mother in an awful fix.
What I'm doing with mother is pointing out to her
that she is making the transitional step from good
mother of the past, and good wife of the past; she's
got to look forward to that era in life in which her
children are grown up. She now occupies the position
of expectant grandmother. Not a wife. Not a mother.
But the expectant grandmother, in that she can now
expect her sons to marry and father children. That expectant grandmother role of hers is so vaguely defined. How does one define it? She's quite pleased with
it. She's working on it. I think she's going to solve her
resentment about her husband taking that teaching
job for the summer because she's got the much more
important role to work on — expectant grandmotherhood. But there's nothing *real* enough about the
grandmotherhood to cause her any immediate trouble. The whole thing is so vague, and yet so seriously
stated to her, and so plausible and so reasonable that
it can take up all of her fantasies.

H: Well, when you see a family like that I gather you don't
see them all together?

E: I've seen this family all together, and then I've seen
them separately.

H: How do you handle them when you're all together with
them? I mean, do you lecture them, or do you get
them interacting with each other, or how do you manage?

E: In order to build up the situation with *this* family, I had
to tell mother that she must prepare herself for an ut-

terly unusual situation. Then I had her place her hands in her lap, I think it was essentially this way, so that she could look at her palms. And I told her to feel her hands there very carefully and to keep looking at them. Keep the thumbs just about that far apart. Not this close, not that far away, but just about like that, and to feel the weight of her hand. And that she would then have an exceedingly hard struggle keeping her mouth shut. And to do it no matter what her son said. No matter what her husband said. Then I turned to the husband and I told him that he would have to keep his mouth shut. And I told the oldest son to keep his mouth shut. The second son to keep his mouth shut. That allowed the baby of the family, who was the least important one, the one whose opinions were least momentous, to start voicing his opinions of each of the other members of the family. As they listened to him tolerantly, and especially mother, she could curb her lip, because that was just the baby, not understanding very much, talking. Mother thereby affirmed the second son's and the first son's right to talk. Then, of course, she would affirm the husband's right to talk.

H: You proceeded this way with each of them?

E: With the whole group. Third son, second son, first son, father, then mother. In order to have the last say, she had to keep her mouth shut. That meant if she were to answer all those things, and have the last say, she had to listen attentively. Now and then I'd raise the question, "Are you really listening to that, mother? Because how will you be able to reply if you don't listen?" So she was horribly trapped.

W: The mothers we've been dealing with, it would take a whale of a trap to hold them still.

H: Why did you tie the hands in with it?

E: Well, you have to tie them together some way. If they

maintain *this*, then the tendency is to keep the mouth shut. (Demonstrating holding the thumbs slightly apart)

W: Sort of a parallel.

E: Sort of a parallel. It holds them. In order to get up out of the chair, see what they've got to do? (Moves the hands) This keep them from initiating any adverse activity, because they first have to undo this, and this is so unimportant. There's no reason why it should be undone. But before they can do *anything*, they've got to undo that, and keeping the thumbs just so far apart. Not this way, not this way, but like this. They can always correct the tendency to put the thumbs together. Every time they correct it, they cooperate.

H: Did you do this for one session, or several, or what?

E: I had several sessions.

H: Each time the same set up starting with the youngest?

E: After I once started with the son, the youngest, then I think the second . . . let's see, I had three sessions with the group. I started with the father the second time, because he's actually the weakest member of the group, because he's been bullied all his life. His mother started out by bullying him, then his foster mother, and then the orphanage bullied him, and he married a wife who had continued it.

H: Did you see them individually first to take a history like that?

E: The father came to see me to find out if I'd be willing to see the members of his family, and he came secretly without letting his wife know. He said he was too unhappy and too miserable and his sons were getting into trouble with the law. He had been analyzed years before by Eisler. He's not a Phoenix patient. He's from out of Phoenix. So he went for a drive one day, landed in Phoenix, so his wife didn't even know he was here.

H: What you tend to do when you see the family together is to restrict their communication there?

E: You restrict it by building up the restriction so that they are motivated to be more communicative. It's just temporary restriction. Because you listen to Little Johnny, and then to Medium Willy, and Big Tom and then hubby. Well each one motivates the other to be more communicative because he's entitled to that. When it became mother's turn to tell, she literally had to tell everything.

W: This becomes, in a way, the opposite of what these families ordinarily do, as I see it, which is to talk a great deal without saying anything.

E: That's right. You see, mother, in the ordinary situation, can talk by the hour, and never succeed in saying a thing. But in that situation she had to have plenty to say on every point that Little Johnny, Medium Willy, Big Tom and Bigger Joe had to say. And everything about herself. And everything about her father, and her mother, and her aunt and uncle and so on. It was utterly amazing the amount of information.

H: Are there other ways that you restrict them, like this? I remember once you proposed a game of cards as another way. Do you have other devices?

E: Yes. When you've got a group situation, you restrict the wife from looking at her husband.

W: From looking at him?

E: Yes. Restrict the husband from looking at his wife. They feel that restriction very, very strongly. There's always tendencies to sneak a look and see how the other person's taking it. But that's the naughty thing to do. That's their reaction to that. So they have to spill much more than they ever thought of spilling. That need to do something. They can't quite do it, and they've got to do something, and all they *can* do is communicate.

H: Verbally, you mean?

E: Verbally. Because they can't sneak that look, and they feel guilty about sneaking that look, you see, and therefore they express ideas and thoughts and tell things that carry a burden of guilt. So you've just created a nice guilt-producing situation so that they will communicate other guilt. However, with that sort of thing, you have to watch and make certain that they don't use it for vengeance. They start recriminations, "He wouldn't take me out to dinner." You don't want that. That's just fault-finding.

W: It seems to me that in some of the families we've been dealing with, at least the one I've been thinking of that I see all together, I have actually been provoking some recrimination and I wonder if you think that it is or is not in order against background which we have in this family. Despite the fact that they are obviously miserable — he has ulcers and she drinks like a fish, one boy is in the mental hospital here — they come in and, sitting all together, present the picture: "Everything is dandy between us and we agree on everything." In this situation, certainly a considerable part of *my* effort has been to get them to speak up a little about what is not so dandy.

E: Well, I think recrimination is a good thing, but I enlarge upon the recrimination then. I want mother, I want brother, I want father to be very, very sure not to tell something that father would prefer mother and brother didn't learn about. In other words, I make father very watchful of his utterances. I make mother very watchful of her utterances. And brother very watchful of his. But while they are watchful of their own utterances, they are extremely watchful of the other person. Because he might betray himself. I have suggested that you better be watchful of what you say unless you betray yourself. Now mother is going to watch her statements, but she's going to see how father and brother are going to betray themselves. So you get, not recriminations, but resentments, because mother's going to watch for father to betray himself on some of her unhappy ideas.

W: Well, aren't you there, sort of thinking over what they must have been doing already? I mean, if they're anything like the ones I've seen, while appearing offhand, they're watchful as hell.

E: Yes. But you're taking it over, and you're demanding that they do that. You are forcing them to do the things that they were going to do anyway out of *your* range of activity. Now just like the farmer who puts up signs, "All hunters welcome," and then he says, "Yes, you're welcome, I'll show you where the pasture is; keep away from it." So he sends them hunting where they should be hunting. He's protecting his pasture. He could put up "No trespassing" signs, and they'd sneak into the pasture and every other place. The farmer's taking control of that. Guiding it and directing it.

H: One of the things you're also doing is preventing an alliance against *you*.

E: Yes.

H: You've got them watching each other.

E: That's right.

H: How much do you deliberately work to break up an entente? I mean, a couple obviously have problems with each other, but they come to you and they present a relatively united front.

E: Therefore you need to break that up without seeming to break it up. A man and his wife, it's a rather simple thing, because you can tell the wife, while the husband sits there and smiles smugly to himself, "You know you really have to make it rather simple when you explain things to me, because, being a man, I can't really understand the subtleties." What does she do? She steps on the other side of the fence right away, isn't that right? Because she is going to differentiate herself as a female, and I'm a poor, miserable male. Her husband is going to recognize that I'm an intelligent male, and that I really understand the masculine side, and he steps over and joins me. I've got that all busted up right there.

W: Suppose you then wish to keep the division but get over on the wife's side, how would you go about that?

E: Well, you use the ploy – I suddenly become not a poor, dumb, stupid male, I become the interested third party who's not involved in this. Then I'm on both sides of the fence. I'm on his, but I'm also on hers. Being a third party, objectively interested, I can really understand the woman's side much better. Before, I emphasize that as a male I don't understand very much, but as the third party, objectively, and only objectively interested, then I can really understand it. So I have a dual role – the stupid male and an intelligent, objective observer. You see, that gives the woman, at any time, the opportunity of doing it either way. Now if she wants to view me as stupid, then she's going to compensate for that by crediting me with intelligence, because she just isn't going to waste her time on a completely stupid man. She came to me because I'm an intelligent, objective person. You see, my stupidity gives her the opportunity to reject, and in return for giving her permission to reject, she is then under obligation to receive.

W: Since she has a mixed attitude about you, if you emphasize one side of it, she's got to emphasize the other.

E: That's right. Because why should I assume the responsibility of maintaining all the equilibrium? As I start rocking the boat this way, well then she's going to lean this way.

W: The same thing goes, only, "You've got to make it simple for me," forces her to come out more into the open.

E: That's right. It also implies if she makes it simple for me, that she can simplify complex things, and thus is not revealing *all* because it's just the simple aspects.

H: One of the other mixtures is I feel, and I think John does too, that we're in a sort of halfway house between what is usually called insight therapy and the kind of directive therapy you do. I'm always caught not quite doing either very completely. Here's an example; I wonder how you would deal with it. You have a child, say a schizophrenic, or anybody, and the parents and the child are caught in this horrible relationship, with the main problem being the child can't get with them, but he also can't get away from them. Every time he starts to get away, they pull him back. Now I don't think *you* would handle this by discussing this with them or pointing it out to them. Or, when they started to pull him back, you wouldn't point out to them just what they're doing. You would handle it in some other way, is that right?

E: Well, they're going to pull the child toward them when the child is trying to get away, and then when the child tries to get *to* them they push him away.

W: Absolutely.

E: Therefore, I would like to disorient them so that when the child is trying to get away, they push him away.

H: How do you do this?

E: Getting that third son to move in with the older brother; every time the mother told me, "But you don't understand me," I immediately emphasized that as long as son three was at home, she'd have an opportunity to understand *him*. I did that over and over again. Every time she mentioned that I *didn't* understand *her*, I pointed out that she could understand her *son*, since he was living at home. Every time she admitted that I *did* seem to understand her in some regard, I mentioned, "You know this idea of your son living with his brother, I haven't made up my mind about that." So every time I understood her, I mentioned the possibility of brother living with brother. Every time she said I didn't understand her, I mentioned son living with *her*. And therefore, since I didn't understand her, I was always saying the thing that was wrong; I didn't understand her. What was I saying when I didn't understand her? Son living with you. Every time she said I understood, I spoke about brother living with brother. And I disapproved of brother living with brother every time she accused me of misunderstanding.

H: From the practical point of view, she says to you, you don't understand me in relation to something that's been going on before, and then all of a sudden you bring up her son living at home. Is that the way it occurs?

E: Yes.

H: Doesn't she feel rather disjointed for a moment? I mean, doesn't she say, "What the devil has that got to do with you not understanding me?"

E: Yes, but put sufficiently earnestly, she's got to try to find her meaning. And it was mother who literally made brother go to live with brother.

W: On the disjointed point, if you take such a woman and try to talk to her in a very sensible, connective way, she'll disjoint the thing herself.

E: She'll disjoint it. And if there's any disjointing to be done, I'd prefer to do it. (Laughter)

H: Then what you would do is try to define the leaving as a coming to? That is, at the moment I'm thinking about getting a schizophrenic girl separated from her parents and boarding out in a foster home, more or less. The way you would handle that would be to define this as being done under the parents' protection so that she wasn't leaving them, but in actual physical movement she'd be 40 miles from them.

E: Yes. This mother is actually glad *she* thought of brother living with brother. The father and the three brothers are still wondering how I managed to make mother force the issue of brother living with brother. Because mother has discredited me, but fortunately she's sufficiently in command of the situation so that the right things are being done. I haven't got much hope for the mother. I have for the other four members of the family.

H: I've gathered that before, in a couple of cases you mentioned with the mother of a schizophrenic, you don't seem to feel there is much hope for them.

E: They are so tremendously bound up and they are so unwilling to recognize it.

H: Is it the schizophrenic you're speaking of, or the mother of a schizophrenic who is bound up?

E: Well, if mother is a schizoid personality.

H: The difficulty with them that we see is this unfortunate way they have of whatever way you go they have to go the opposite. That isn't necessarily useful, because if you then start going to the opposite they go the other way at that point. But this works very rapidly. That is, they aren't just negativistic. A negativistic person you can push in the opposite direction.

W: I wonder if it isn't something a little bit like my saying to the family something about the way for their son to be independent is to get together with him? This boy was still pretty schizy. He brings up the idea, "All I want to do is go out and get married." I suggest to him that while this is a nice aim, that in order to really do it he should get together with his family first.

H: Now this is a larger point we're concerned about: Whether it's necessary for a schizophrenic. . . . I

mean, you can take a schizophrenic and take him
away from his parents and he can still be as schizy
as the devil, or you move him through therapy away
from his parents and he may move pretty slowly.
Whether it's useful, or perhaps necessary, and possible, to take him back into the family and require him
to learn to handle his parents, as a way of getting free
from the problems he has.

E: Can he really learn to handle his parents?

H: It's a question.

E: He's got a lifetime of experience in which he has learned
not to handle them.

W: That sure is true.

E: He's learned such a wealth of tiny little ways, and such
tiny little skills in not handling his parents.

H: Your first impulse then is to get them separate, as fast
as possible?

E: Get them separated. When mother begins to recognize
that you've outmaneuvered her in getting sonny outside the family, then you defeat mother in another
way at another level. Because she is really going to
get sonny back into her clutches. Because while she
had to go opposite of you, when she discovers that
you want her to go opposite of you, then she's right
along with you. But that's when you frustrate her
completely by flatly, absolutely, refusing to discuss
the matter. She can't do anything about getting sonny
back to the home until she first discusses it with you
and makes you admit that you were in error. And you
are refusing to discuss it.

H: He has attitudes about women, or men, and so on, built
in to him by his parents and carries these attitudes
away, and this is again an insight problem. That a kid
can get away from his parents but not really be away
from them — "I've been away from them 372 days and
three hours" — that sort of thing.

E: Yes.

H: Is it wiser under those circumstances to bring the kid back with his parents so that he leaves them feeling more free?

E: I know, but you get the kid away from his parents, and you get him all set to discover the identity of somebody else in his environment. That is, you get the girl out of her parental home, and she's got an apartment. She goes to sleep with the idea, the feeling, that she's still at home and papa and mama are in the next room asleep. She isn't really away from her parents. But you pose the problem of finding out in how many ways the landlady and the landlord are different from her father and mother. The landlady and the landlord, well, they're cruder people. They talk with poor English. They're pretty graspy; they're not generous. They're not thoughtful. And pretty soon the concept comes, "But they do leave you alone." Then you've got maybe the opening wedge inserted. Then they start identifying *other* people. Then you simply build up the identity of this other person, and that person, and the first thing they know, they have built up some relationships with other people. The more relationships you build up with other people, the more you adulterate father and mother relationships.

H: By identifying other people, you mean differentiating this person from all others?

E: That's right. That girl moved into an apartment at my request and always went to sleep at night in her bed feeling very strongly – and she said it was so unreal, and yet it was so real – papa and mama were in the next room sleeping. She could almost hear them snoring. She could almost hear them turn over in bed.

W: You instructed her to feel that?

E: No, that was her reaction. So she hadn't really moved away from them. Then my demand that she identify her landlady and her landlord. It's a simple problem – an identification of two specimens of the human race.

The landlady was so tall and weighed approximately so much, and the landlord was so tall and weighed approximately so much. He had a moustache. Until she began to look upon them not as just physical objects but as living human beings.

W: But you start on them as different physical objects.

E: As different physical objects. Then she got more and more extensive in her identification. She had to drag in personal qualities. The landlady had a much nicer voice than her mother.

H: Why is it that you wouldn't, with the mother, discuss with her, and point out to her, her difficulties in letting the child get away?

E: When does a child leave the mother?

W: I sometimes wonder.

E: I know. But with that type of mother, the child, so far as her willingness to think about it, that child leaves the mother only when the minister says, "I now pronounce you man and wife." He moves out into marriage, into another home, with another woman. But not until that moment can she conceive of the child moving out. There's no possibility of that happening, because Sonny isn't even in love. It will probably be several years before he gets engaged. Of course, he ought to have at least a year-long courtship, or longer. She's perfectly willing that he gets married way off in the dim and distant future, so she never had to crystalize the idea of Sonny leaving her. But Sonny is leaving her by virtue of entering into his teens. Up to puberty he's *her* little baby, and as soon as he gets into the teens he starts leaving. Before puberty he's just her baby, an undifferentiated human being. But as soon as he enters puberty, then he becomes very definitely a male. And a different male. And a male destined for some other female. So he starts to leave, but the schizy mother can conceptualize that matter

of leaving only as the outcome of a marriage ceremony, which is definitely in the future.

W: You emphasize the ceremony there, I think?

E: That's right. She emphasizes the ceremony.

W: Specifically she can't see the relationship, she can only
see the form.

E: Only the form.

*   *   *

H: Well, the most typical parent-child problem that we see
is the inability of the parents to draw any line with
the child because the child won't like it. This terrible
feeling of "the child will leave me forever if I punish
him in any way."

E: What do they need to be told?

H: That's what I would like to know.

E: "The child will leave you forever. Why would a child
leave you forever? Of course, he's going to, you know.
But why would he leave you forever? Of course, he's
going to, you know. Of a certainty, but why would
he?" I ask that question repetitiously without giving
a chance to answer. "The child will leave you because
you didn't do the right thing. But of course the child
is going to leave you anyway, whether you do the
right thing or the wrong thing. Of course you do want
the child to leave you because you want your son to
grow up and move away and live with another woman.
And cleave unto her, abandoning all others, including
you."

H: They're not usually that explicit about, "They'll leave me
forever," but that seems to be the feeling they have.
They chastise the child and then the child is unhappy
because he's been chastised, and they can't stand it.
Then they go and they make it up in some way.

E: Yes. So those parents should be made to realize by the
analogy, "What do you want the dentist to do when

your child has an aching tooth? Just give the child
some medicine to cover up the pain, or do you want
the dentist to hurt the child? Because no matter how
much local anesthetic is given, remember the needle
will hurt. Remember, there'll be a cavity in the jaw.
Remember, there'll be a tenderness as the jaw heals.
What do you want the doctor to do about that great
big painful boil? Don't you want the doctor to shove
a knife through it quickly and hurt the child horribly
for a second?"

W: So you use an analogy to bring in the idea of the hurt
that really fixes something up.

E: The hurt that fixes.

*   *   **

H: I mean it this way. I have a mother and she has a
daughter, and her constant complaint is, "When does
a mother stop being a mother? How long am I going
to take care of my daughter?" Daughter is in and out
of the mental hospital. "How long am I going to have
this burden?" She's very resentful of this burden. I'm
sure she hasn't much awareness at all that she can't
let the girl get away. Now you wouldn't discuss with
her her difficulties in letting the girl get away, I
gather. The girl went away to college at about 18, had
a rough time the first quarter, began to do better the
second quarter, and her mother decided to go back to
college, or go to college. She went down and joined
her.

E: Mmm hmm.

H: The girl cracked up that summer.

E: Mmm hmm.

H: Now several psychiatrists have told this mother she
contributed to the crack up by her going down to the
college. The mother's response to this is, "I'm not go-

ing to quit school." The mother is continuing school, and the daughter's in the hospital. She really can't understand, I don't think, why they connect this in any way, because she can't see the fact that she's holding her daughter. All she can see is she's trying to get rid of the girl. "And I wish she'd get well and get away from me," Now, once again, on this insight problem, I gather you wouldn't work to help her discover, learn, or whatever, that she isn't letting that girl get away?

E: I know. One of the procedures that I employed, and I have employed, is this matter of questioning some of these overly possessive mothers about the daughters' growth and development. With the mother, if it would be at all possible, I'd raise with her the question, "Do you want this girl to establish herself as an independent creature? You have quite rightly so expressed that as your desire. But there are a number of things that you'll have to tell me to help me understand what's wrong with the girl that she hasn't seemed to be willing to leave you. Now, when the girl was growing, when she was a little girl, and then entered into puberty, what was the first thing about the girl's pubertal changes that the girl brought to your attention? Did she alter the way she moved her chest? Did she sort of bring her pelvis to your attention? Did she in some way manage to take a bath and need some towels that she forgot, so that she could let you know that she was growing pubic hair? Just what was her attitude toward lipstick? Was she willing to learn, from you, the importance of utilizing to the fullest her lip contour?" Then I'd take that mother, systematically, through all the steps, the changing steps of pubertal growth and development. Always emphasizing the daughter as a different person. And the bewilderment the mother had because the daughter was actually interested in a totally different kind of personality. Until mother would have a tremendous sense that she didn't belong in her daughter's class in college, she didn't belong on her daughter's campus. That her daughter belongs to another, younger, new generation. But you see, I'd be emphasizing the growth of the daughter, and the fact that mother is fully established as an adult, mature, female. And that she is watching the increased appearance of pubic hairs. Watching the increased growth of her daughter's breasts. A breast that is going to be meaningful to another man than father. You get these schizophrenic mothers who get along perfectly all right until the child starts to enter puberty, and then it's such a shocking experience for the mother.

H: You wouldn't suggest to the mother, or discuss with her, her difficulties in letting the child go?

E: No, because that's her reaction to it. To the ceremony of letting go. But I let the mother get awfully, painfully, acutely aware of the fact that daughter is growing up. That daughter is adding one pubic hair after another. Daughter is adding one bra size after another. That daughter is appealing to, first the 15-year-old boy, then the 16, then the 17, then the 18-year-old boy. And that daughter isn't really appealing to mature men the way mother is. And if daughter is appealing to, and interested in, only immature boys, that emphasizes that mother has her superior experience, and her superior maturity, and her interest in *mature* men. The mother is differentiating herself. She's being forced to the conclusion that daughter may be fish but she is fowl. (Laughter)

W: That's what you're offering mother in exchange for the realization that daughter is not a part of her anymore.

E: Yes. Because who wants to hang on to the fish when you really are a bird?

H: Well, again the difference in approach. I think, what

do you think in terms of the function . . . now it seems apparent to us that these mothers and fathers, in some sense, need a burden that they gain from the kid being schizophrenic. That they somehow . . . for example, at the crudest level, they might fight a good deal more or they might separate if they didn't have a sick child. This holds them together. That they gain like that in quite a number of ways so that it's very hard for them to let the child get healthy and go about his business. Now how do you handle . . . I mean, this is again a problem, to some extent, of insight. There are two schools functioning here that I'm still trying to differentiate in my mind.

E: Father and mother are sticking together and hanging on to child.

W: Meanwhile blaming any difficulties on the mentally ill child.

E: That's right, and the child is so very, very useful.

H: "We would be so happy if Burt wasn't sick." They will state that they have no other difficulties except that.

E: And sick sonny or sick daughter is the *only* bone of contention. Their only frustration in life. Again, I go through that developmental process, and I can introduce that threat, "You can wonder about when your son reaches *your* age whether he is going to have the same trouble with *his* children." You've actually accused them of having a future of being grandparents. They've got to resolve son's difficulties all the way along the line up to the point where they become grandparents. But they are accepting the idea of a change in themselves. When you can get them to think about being grandparents, we can think about what kind of a grandmother would she make? She starts thinking the same thing. They haven't seen that coming. Then you've got them started on an examination of their views of each other. To deal with that, they have to get sonny somewhere where he can provide a grandchild for them so that they can deal with her deficiencies as a grandmother, and she can deal with his deficiencies as a grandfather, but they better shove sonny out into the cold world where he can get married and sire a child so they can actually fight that issue out.

H: You mean in the anticipation of that fight, they can go a period of years?

E: Oh yes.

H: We find, related to this same problem, that if the kid does get better, there's quite a disturbance in the family. Mother gets upset. Father gets upset. They may fight more. There's a possibility, or certainly the mother seems to feel, that she's going to have a breakdown.

E: I can think of two very, very possessive schizoid parents. Horribly so. When their daughter went to college, well of course mother did all the laundry for daughter, all the sewing, mother supervised all the weekends. Of course, a girl that goes to college is likely to encounter young men. Likely to fall in love. In that schizoid fashion they approved of it. They even built on rooms in that house for daughter and her husband to live. They were really going to run that girl's life, including the life of her husband that she picked up. My approach to the matter, when they built on the rooms and started furnishing them for their daughter's anticipated falling in love, anticipated engagement, anticipated marriage, was to fall in line. I anticipated daughter's pregnancy. And daughter's delivery. And grandson's crying. And grandson's learning to walk. And to the anticipated grandmother, I anticipated grandfather's lack of understanding of his grandson. To anticipated grandfather, I anticipated grandmother's lack of understanding.

It wound up with the two of them insisting when daughter really did get married, that daughter go to

Tucson to live. They both consulted me about how often I thought the other was entitled to visit. My statement to Grandpa was that Grandma ought not to visit oftener than one afternoon every six weeks or two months. And by curious coincidence, I felt the same about Grandpa. So they've been visiting about one afternoon every six weeks or two months.

The daughter was very much alarmed about her parents. She asked me about, "What're they going to do to me? Building on an addition to the house so that if I ever fall in love, if I ever get engaged, if I ever get married, that I have to live there?" I told her fall in line with it. I'll handle this. Those two parents are still complimenting me on my wisdom. And Grandpa is seeing to it that Grandma is not too solicitous.

W: You've got each one controlling the other one.

E: And taking a tremendous joy in their grandchild and their daughter and her husband. They've got a controlled situation. But you know it *was* a question: How would grandson learn to walk in those rooms? What kind of a grandparent would the spouse be? That theoretical speculation. On Grandma being too solicitous, Grandpa being too solicitous. And daughter is just a freshman in college. She didn't get married until her senior year. Yet I went through this question of grandson while daughter was a freshman. Because part of her high school graduation present was the building on of a room with the plans for more rooms. As the daughter grew up, she and her husband would live right there.

W: So once again you fell into line and took it over.

E: Yes. I went so much further down the line than they could comprehend, and I helped them build so elaborately that they had to build for that oversolicitous grandparent.

H: Well really, you do a kind of substitution, then, of the idea "grandparents" for the idea "mother or father"?

E: That's right. But isn't it a legitimate substitution?

H: Yes.

E: Because parent can't remain parent forever. The new mother has to change into an older and older and older mother. You can't tell her that she's got to change.

H: And your goal isn't in any way to get the mother one day when walking down the street to realize, "I've been holding on to this daughter and not letting her get away"?

E: Well, that's an offensive idea. It would give her an increased amount of guilt.

H: I'm talking about what is meant by insight, discovery. Oh, you mean guilt about having done it?

E: About having done it. If you can correct the issue without the mother suffering such extreme guilt – well, think of these grandparents. Why should they ever feel guilty about that addition they put on the house? In their old age as grandparents they've got two alternatives: one to keep that in case daughter or husband or grandchild wants to come and visit for a long visit; or they can rent it out to tenants and have an increased income, and they're going to leave their savings to daughter and her child. Now why should they feel so horribly guilty about that addition to the house? It's a perfectly sound thing. They *are* renting that. Why should they feel guilty about it? You and I can look at that addition to that house and think what an awful thing for parents to do. To grow up visualizing the daughter as such a helpless appendage, with no rights, no privileges, whose entire future is dictated, and here is the tangible evidence of the extent of that dictation. We can see it as horrible. The parents can look upon it as a nice source of extra income that goes into a savings account that will probably help educate grandson. Well, which is better? Is it essential that they feel guilt? I don't believe in salvation only through pain and suffering.

H: Well, you'd only work for insight with parents, it seems to me, in order to prevent some future grasping by the mother of the child. This undermining, constant undermining. I mean, here's a typical example: A patient here wants to go home on trial visit. The mother starts talking to him about how he ought to be more independent. Another week he says he's on the hospital baseball team, he's going to go down to Moffet Field down here and play with the team. She said, "That's fine, dear, there are doctors there too." So there is this constant kind of undermining influence whenever he does begin to get independent. Now, if they continue to have contact with each other, and the mother doesn't have any awareness of his difficulty, she's going to continue to undermine him.

E: I know, but she's had a lifetime of experience in not having insight. You can give her insight into her behavior in one particular regard, or a dozen regards, but will she have insight into another type of behavior that's just as restrictive? You teach the mother, "You don't use toilet paper on your son for him. Let him wipe his own bottom. He's ten years old, you know. (Laughter) Let him walk across the street. It's a residential section, there's no traffic there, and he's ten years old, you know. He's old enough to walk across the street. Let him go to school all by himself. The traffic patrol there will take care of him crossing the streets safely. Let him go to the toilet in the schoolhouse." And so on. You can give the mother absolute insight into all those things. What is that poor kid doing? Mother is very helpful with his career as a musician. He is studying music and he's very gifted, but mother is guiding and guiding and guiding him on every note and every piece of music.

H: You don't think, then, that she generalizes from wiping his rear end to the music?

E: You just can't make her understand. Of course, mother

has had musical training. Mother has had much more experience. This is a learning situation. Mother does have perfect pitch, and she knows so much about music, having graduated from the Boston Conservatory. And had excellent teachers, and being gifted herself. But, nevertheless, it's not a teacher's role that she has. It's mother helping her little boy. The excellence with which she arranged the music on the piano was just as delicate as the way she used the toilet paper on his rear. When he picks up his violin, she takes hold of his arm with the same care that she held his arm when walking across the street. But you can't tell that to her. *This* is different. But it's the same thing. And there's no way of her recognizing that.

H: It's strange that you assume this about the mother when in the patients you treat you assume that, if you get them to do one thing, they will generalize to others.

E: That's right, because you're only dealing with the patient. With the mother, you've got two patients there. And the mother is bringing the son. You give her insight. You're trying to get sonny straightened out. Mother knows it's sonny that needs to be straightened out. Of course, she isn't too much at fault, and she isn't really your patient, and so she has the privilege of going back. If I can have the mother, only, as the patient, I would like to get her fighting with her husband.

H: Then what?

E: Then she'd let sonny alone. Because she hates her husband.

H: I've got a mother fighting with her husband, and she still won't leave the daughter alone.

W: Husband doesn't fight back.

H: If he gets drunk he does. They get drunk every weekend and fight.

E: Have you differentiated the daughter from the father?

H: I've been trying to bring them together.

E: I mean, you say the mother fights with her husband but still picks on her daughter. But, of course, in fighting with father, she can also fight with father through the daughter, because the daughter is equated with the father in certain ways. At least 50 percent of the daughter is father, isn't that right? If you differentiate the daughter as no part of the father, then she's got to fight with father here, but here's daughter over here now, which way is she going to direct her energies? Because this daughter really isn't part of father. In other words, you differentiate the daughter so completely from the father.

W: I think we've got to be going.

*   *   *

1961. Present were Milton H. Erickson, Jay Haley, and John Weakland.

W: When treating a family or a couple, what, if anything, are the really crucial things to start changing? In other words, you sometimes speak of getting a wedge into the situation, but is there anything that is central to change compared with other things?

E: Almost always I insist right away on the recognition of the integrity of the individual as a completely separate person.

E: Well, I would take this as meaning that you want to unlock them a little from each other?

E: That's right. Even with the five-year-old, even with the two-year-old—you can't communicate much to the two-year-old—but you can get the father and the mother to recognize that the two-year-old is another person. Then, of course, if there are two kids in the family, you point out to the father and mother that they are absolutely unrelated to each other. She comes from one ancestral background, and he comes from another, and they are not blood relatives in any sense of the word. The brother and sister, and the two sisters, are decidedly closely related. They are made up of two bloodstreams, identical bloodstreams. One of which is alien to the mother. One of which is alien to the father. Therefore, they better recognize that their children are separate individuals, because of that mixture of different bloodstreams, one of which is alien to her and one of which is alien to her husband. The separateness and individuality of the child is assured at the biological level. Then you point out that you inherit just so much from your parents, so much from your grandparents, and so much from your great-grandparents, and that your parents are merely a vehicle of transmission of inheritance. That's why in a family of eight kids you have eight completely different individuals, all different.

I can think of one family that appalled me. A very brilliant young man married this very delightful young woman, and they've got a family of five children. I visited in the home when the oldest child was 15. It was a Saturday, father was home, mother was home, the children were home, and they were really having a family day. Even though I was visiting there, they had their family day. They did it by sitting down in the livingroom, and they all sat there and listened while mother and father took turns reading a story book to little Johnny, aged five. The 15-year-old sat there and listened to the story that was read to Johnny, and the 13-year-old, and the 11-year-old. After they read several stories to little Johnny, all of them listening and sharing a togetherness, they, with togetherness, went out into the backyard, each with a little shovel, and they each dug a hole in the backyard, because little Johnny wanted to dig a hole. That is a complete togetherness at the minimal level. Now I will agree that was a family in which there was no quarreling, no disagreements. But it was an appalling family. I don't know how you would describe it. These were college educated parents. Were they malicious? I don't think they were consciously. I don't think there was any malice of forethought. I don't see how they could be that stupid. But the 15-year-old, and the 13-year-old, and the 11-year-old—utterly featureless as individuals. The 15-year-old had to listen to the 13-year-old and the 11-year-old.

W: I think this is particularly striking to me, because I've been working for quite a while with a family with a badly schizophrenic child where the mother is a native Californian and the father is a native born European. It's just been dawning more and more on me that even in this family where there are conflicts about their differences, or ostensibly about their differences, actually I've gotten much further when I said, "Yes, of course you're different," than I ever did before. Even when they're already quarreling about the differences, to emphasize the fact that of course they are different is helpful in that it frees them from each other some.

E: Yes, that's right. You separate them, and then you give them the opportunity for an overall appraisal. What *is* so different, and what do I like about that difference, what can I use about that difference.

W: That was very hard to see when they were already quarreling about the difference, but it still applied.

E: I think I've mentioned to you another technique I have for warring families. I can think of the father and the mother and the daughter, and I set the clock. I gave them a statement, "age before beauty, ladies first." The mother had the first 20 minutes in which to lay out her daughter, and lay out her husband, while they sat there gritting their teeth and keeping their mouths shut. The daughter came next, and she really tore into her mother. Just laid her out. Then she tore into her father, and then father's turn. Then the question, "Now how much, mother, did you agree with what your husband said about daughter? How much did you agree about what your daughter said about your husband?" But this polite listening in silence while the other is free to say anything, and as exaggeratedly as possible—I've staged that sort of quarrel in the office repeatedly.

*   *   *

E: Another variation: "I'm going to listen to each one of you and see what you really do mean. I'm going to keep my mouth shut, and my eyes and ears open, so that I can see and hear what *you* mean. So mother, for the next 15 minutes, just blast away at four of the most courteous listeners there are. Pull no punches. Give them a chance to listen and to see what you actually mean. Then after you, mother, I think father should. Then after father, I think brother should, because he's older than sister. I think the three of you ought to teach the youngest member of the family quite a bit about listening and hearing and understanding." I will let mother blast all through them, and I listen to it with the greatest of interest and curiosity. Father kept looking over at me, and I *was* listening. He did his level best to listen intelligently. Brother and sister were watching father watching me, and you could see written all over brother's face, "I can do it better than father." And he did. And sister's delight at seeing father and mother and brother at their worst as they each took their turn. Then you could see that grin on sister's face, triumphant, the last word. But she was the youngest, and the most incompetent for the last word. But I knew that; she didn't. But she had absolute freedom. And that was the way I handled that particular family difficulty. They came in fairly often for a couple of months for a family tearing down and building up. And finally they were building up good family relationships. "Sticks and stones may break my bones, but names will never hurt me," was one way which I summarized one of those interviews.

C H A P T E R 3

Dealing with the
Difficult Family

1958. Present were Milton H. Erickson, Gregory Bateson, Jay Haley, and John Weakland.

H: On the question of families, particularly the kind of severe families we deal with — they're the kind that anything you do is wrong, and anything any member of the family does is wrong, and nothing can get very definite and nothing can get very set anyway. Now, how do you handle this in a directive way — where inevitably directions aren't going to be followed? If you give a clear statement, they aren't going to do it, that's all.

E: Give me an example.

B: Father and mother had been married 19 years, and during the whole of that time she has battled for control of the salary check. Her right as a woman had been infringed. Shortly before they came to us he capitulated, gave her the salary check, and took on a second job to try and redeem the family finances. Incidentally, she indirectly confessed to having been sabotaging the household financial system, not economizing the way she knew she could have. And he's quite obviously been sabotaging the finances on his side, be-

52

cause it paid them both! She demonstrates in this way that he's inadequate. Shortly following his giving her this salary check, the boy raises such hell at school —the boy has been a long time near schizo, now 15, and he immediately gets turned out of school. They wouldn't have anything to do with him anymore, which brings the family to us. At the end of the first session, talking about this salary check business, the father makes a very straight, but a little bit withdrawn, statement on the following lines, "Yes I have altered that. I agreed that it was a great mistake I made to try and keep the control in my hands. I think that my reasons for saying that this is a mistake are different from yours." Wife: "You're just being facetious."

E: "And your wife says that you are being facetious, and you know you're not."

B: This would be your reply?

E: That's my statement. "All right, but your wife says you are facetious and you know that you are not. Your wife says you are, and you know that you are not. Now one of you *ought to be* right. Ladies first. You tell her that you are not *right*. And you can be not right, and indicate that wheels are going around in your head. You are saying the correct words but this gesture of wheels going around in your head makes those right words facetious words, and your wife is *right*, and you're right too. You're saying the right words." Now what are they going to do with that sort of thing? They have to start looking for other grounds for disagreement. But they're looking for other grounds. You have just provided them with grounds, and they have accepted them, because as soon as they start looking for other grounds, then they have accepted these grounds you just offered him.

I can think of the experimental set-up where two resistant psychology students wanted to go into a trance, but they were completely resistant, and nothing that I did would put them in a trance, so I asked them to face each other. Then I instructed them, "Now you watch the other person very carefully, and be sure not to go into a trance until after he has." And they each had that. "But be sure to go into the trance immediately after he has, but not before he has." So they are obligated to go into a trance after the other. Obligated to go into a trance immediately after the other. And each knows he's going to go into a trance. Each knows the other is going to precede him. Each is keyed to that. That's an impossible situation. They can't go simultaneously.

H: What was their response to this impossible situation?

E: Can you figure it out?

H: Well, the only thing I could guess is that they would go into a trance and deny they were in a trance.

W: Hallucinate that the other person went into a trance?

E: That's *one* way. I was thinking of two in particular. But that's one way they can do it. They can hallucinate the other person going into a trance.

H: What's another way? What else might happen?

E: A withdrawal from the other person. Which is essentially the same as you said—negative hallucination. Find it increasingly difficult to watch the other person. The more difficult it became to judge and observe and watch the other person, the deeper into the trance they went. So they literally withdrew and strengthened their relationship to me.

H: You stayed out of it and just waited?

E: No, I was offering them the suggestions.

H: What sort of suggestions?

E: Trance. To get tired, to get sleepy, slowly to go into a trance, and each watching the other, each getting set to go into a trance just as soon as the other one. With the husband and wife who are at swords' point, you alter the arguments that they use. Wife says he's facetious, you make him facetious. I like to use puns. You say the right words so that by saying the right words, you'll be wrong.

W: I'm lost. Oh, you mean you say the right words as a pun doesn't mean you're right, it means you say the right words?

E: Yes.

H: I was saying to Milton that our families don't follow directions very well, and he was asking for an example. Could you give an example of when you were trying to film this family on Sunday?

W: Well it was pretty chaotic. With the S family it is happening, in a way, over and over again.

B: The S family are these people I've just been talking about.

W: I came in, after leaving them in a room for a couple of moments. I started out by being introduced to the family and I had them sit down and said we'll be ready in a minute or two. I go out for a minute, and meanwhile they are on camera without any further instruction. They don't know they're on camera yet; it hasn't been stated. Then I come in, and ordinarily at that point I pick up the family and talk to them for a couple minutes about being in this photographic situation. I may say that I would naturally feel a little bit uncomfortable and anxious, this is just to sort of sound them out and to let them loosen up if they want to. So I come in with that to this family, and before I can get a word out they started off by taking it right out of my hands and saying, "It's just like TV, where's the prompter, where's the script?" Okay, so I attempt to pick this up, I say, "Okay, I'll do a little prompting and write a little script for you."

B: Who said that?

W: Father said that. I forget their specific response to that, but every attempt I made thereafter to give them a suggestion, a procedure to follow, they did something else. Usually our families don't do that so obviously. But they did it very obviously. My first suggestion again followed our usual routine; I would offer them something to talk about for a few minutes and discuss among themselves, something to get started on. I'd suggest a topic to them, and then I'd give them a few minutes by themselves. Afterwards I'd come back in and talk to them. The suggestion I offered is that they plan something they'd like to do together, say, a trip. They said, "Well, we've just been talking about that before we came here." I said, "Well, fine, then you can go on a little further with it." They stopped talking about going on a trip almost immediately. I then came in and started to give them the next one, which is to play the game of "each play an idea." They hassled around. "I don't play games." This was mother's contribution. They kick things around a little bit. I suggest they can try this anyway. They get started in no sequence, and what do you think they're talking about in about one minute? Somebody says, "Well, what about that trip?" (Laughter) Well, this wasn't the end of it, but that's the general shape of the half-hour I spent with them in front of the camera. Of course this was interspersed with a number of dirty cracks about the situation. Mother said something at one point about, "Well, I don't see why, if you're going to do something like this, you didn't just eavesdrop on one of our regular sessions," meaning one of their interviews with Gregory. "It's a little disconcerting just to be sitting here talking to a black stranger." This is me. (Laughter) I said, "Well, you give me an idea there. If you like that better, perhaps we could arrange to film one of your regular sessions." We've thought about filming therapeutic sessions; we haven't had a good opportunity for it. Well, no, that's no good of course. But this is the way the whole thing ran. Mother was a key figure, but they were all involved in it. Whatever gets started, that's broken off, and they're somewhere else.

E: What do you want me to do—discuss this?

H: I just wonder how you handle that? For example, if you have a mother who says, "I never drink, at least not often, and then only on weekends when I want to be more cheerful." Now how do you deal with these kinds of self-contradictory statements?

E: What do you want brought out?

H: Well, how do you get them so that what they say they affirm instead of deny? So they can reach an agreement and stick to an agreement?

E: Yes. "I never have a drink. Only on weekends, when I want to feel cheerful." Is that the statement?

H: Yes. We find in one of these families that what they say, they contradict. That what anybody else says, they contradict.

W: Only they don't even clearly contradict it.

H: That's right. If father says, "Let's go to the movies," mother will say, "All right," only she'll say it like she doesn't really want to go, or she'll say, "Let's go somewhere else," and he'll say, "Well, I only wanted to go to the movies because I thought the child wanted to go," and the child will say, 'Well, I really don't want to go to the movies," and they have a devil of a time getting to the movies even. It's this kind of self-contradiction, and contradiction of each other. They're constantly in this hassle.

E: But as long as the child is going to contradict father, father is going to contradict mother, and mother is going to contradict the child, and contradict father, it's mutually contradictory. You pose the question going to the movies. Then you take it out of their hands, by saying, "Now mother, tell father you won't go. Now child, tell father you will go, since he invited mother, but tell mother you won't go." Before the child's got that handled, then you tell mother, "Now you tell the child that he's got to go, and you tell father that you won't let the child go."

H: You tell them to do this and you wait until they do it? Is that it?

E: Yes.

B: What happens if they say, "Ridiculous. I know my husband."

E: "You're here, and you're trying to learn something. What it is you want to learn you really don't know. You won't even know it after you've learned it. But it will be a part of you, so you do as I tell you, even though you don't know that you're doing as I tell you."

W: (Laughs) That's wrapping them up.

E: You see, usually you take a nice, polite social attitude toward your patients. You present them with an idea, and if they don't respond to it, if they don't accept it, then your face falls and you get crestfallen. Your chin drops, and you try to restate it. You let them know that your feelings are hurt, and you'd rather they wouldn't have turned you down. Saturday night I was demonstrating child hypnosis. I picked a child out of the audience, and I asked him to come up and sit down. I knew nothing about the child. He was a very large child. From the looks of his face he might be 10 and he might be nine. I just couldn't tell because he was obviously large-boned. So I didn't know. And so I pointed out to the audience, "Now there's one way that you can have this boy go into a trance. You ask him to see those dogs there. David, you look at those dogs." He said, "There aren't any dogs there." I said, "That's right, there aren't any dogs, will you look at the dogs there?" "But there aren't any dogs there." I said, "No, there really aren't any dogs there. Now listen to me carefully, David, I would like to have you see dogs there." And he said, "There aren't any dogs there." I said, "That's right, there aren't any dogs there. What I asked of you was to *see* some dogs there." Then he paused, and he said, "I can't see any dogs there." "So maybe you better try a little harder. See some dogs right there." "I can't see any dogs there." (Getting softer and weaker) "You're trying hard, that's fine, just keep on trying because, it isn't important that you see dogs there, it's just important that you try," and I lifted his arm. He was in a trance state. Why should I be upset by all that contradiction? I know what ideas I'm going to present to the crowd. I know what ideas I'm going to present to the patient. Certainly the patient can dispute those ideas. The patient can argue against them. All I need to do is keep on presenting my ideas until the patient realizes that I'm very, very serious about it. Then the situation changes inexplicably. I can help that change by seeming to agree with the child, "I know there are no dogs there but I want you to *see* dogs there." This allows the child to wonder. "I'd like to have you try harder." But it's your absolute persistence in spite of the contradictions, instead of politely withdrawing and trying another gamble with that script thrown away. You tell the patient, "I hope you won't get tired standing up." The patient looks at you and says, "What's the matter with you, I'm sitting down." "Oh, I know you are, but I hope you won't get tired standing up." "Please talk sense, doctor, I'm sitting down. I'm not standing up, and I won't get tired of standing up." "Yes, I hear you, but please try to understand, don't get tired of standing up." And then they know that I understand *them*, but in some way they just don't understand *me*. (Laughter) And that's all that I want them to grasp. That I understand them, they don't understand me.

W: I can put that in another way. Jay, you know I'd say that he gets across the idea that he can top any contradiction they would pull.

H: Well, now you say to the child, on this movie, "I want you to tell your mother that you won't go, and your father that you will go, and mother I want you to prevent the child from going, and tell your father or husband that you'll let them go."

E: "And now, you know, we can keep right on with that sort of thing, but it goes in a circle, you see. But there are certain understandings that you want to get out of this situation; there are three of you involved, father, mother and child. And there *are* certain understandings you want to get. Certain understandings you need to get from father, certain understandings he needs to get from you. Certain understandings you both need to get from the child. And certain understandings the child needs to get from the two of you. But there are certain understandings you need to get from yourself by talking about and clarifying your ideas. And mother, there are certain understandings you need to get from yourself by expressing your ideas and clarifying them. And sonny, there are certain ideas that you need to get from yourself through talking out your ideas and talking to father and mother. And mother, of course you'll have to talk to father and child, and father you'll have to talk to mother and child." And you've presented that, and what can you do about that? You've emphasized they can clarify their own ideas from their own ideas. You need to get something from father, from mother, from child, from each other, from both of the others.

H: Then, in general – I'm trying to understand what you're getting at here – you would take what they're doing already and impose this upon them.

E: That's right. Impose it upon them. And use that as the foundation. "Father, you are disputing mother and child, child you are disputing mother and father, mother you are disputing father and child, and you can keep right on doing that, but you need to clarify your own ideas through knowing what your own ideas are." You can present the entire thing in slightly different words. "You know, father is in the same position, and father, you know that mother needs to clarify her own ideas by expressing her own ideas, and that will clear her mind." Mother's going to say father has to do that himself. But father's going to agree with you that mother should do it, and the child is going to agree with you that both of them should do it, and you've got an awful lot of agreement right there. "And I don't know which one of you should begin first."

H: Let's take another tack on these families. One of the things we find is that a mother will have this transfer of blame; whatever happened, she didn't do it. Or if she did do it, somebody told her to do it. So she doesn't ever acknowledge affecting anybody adversely. In fact, she really does not acknowledge affecting anybody nicely. She denies what she does. Now, how do you handle that sort of a blame problem? How do you get her to acknowledge it? Naturally, what happens is when she doesn't acknowledge any blame, then the rest of the family blames her, and she feels terribly blamed all the time, while busy defending herself about being at fault.

E: I know. How do you want to make her accept blame? Do you want to make her accept blame by antagonism or by agreement? By antagonizing her, or by forcing her to agree with you gently?

H: Neither way in particular.

E: But it has to be some particular way.

B: Well, we are wanting, I should say, to get to a point

where, when somebody says x, y, z, the question "Who is being blamed?" is not the first question that pops into the mother's mind and into everybody else's mind.

E: Yes. I can think of what I did with one mother in that regard. I said, "Mother, now you have explained the situation: No matter how hard you try, something always happens, or someone always does something, that brings your most carefully laid out plans to grief. It's perfectly obvious that it isn't your fault, and you can recognize that fact. But mother, there is something I'd like to point out to you. I don't know if you have a sense of humor, but I'm going to assume that you do have a sense of humor, and I'm going to ask father to feel your back from one shoulder to the other shoulder. Just straight across your back, to pass his hand from this shoulder to this shoulder. And I want him to tell me what he feels." Father did that, he said he had felt her shoulder blades. I said, "That's quite right, I was very certain you would. Now I don't know what you think about a sense of humor. I don't know how corny you like humor. But I want to point out to you what you've been telling me. No matter how carefully you plan things, either something happens or someone in some way interferes, and upsets your plans, so that you are *perfectly* disappointed every time. And I thought only angels were perfect, and your husband didn't feel any wings. (Laughter) And so you know, really, honest now, I'm not going to believe that you can do things with such perfection. Now if you'll think hard there was some time when you didn't plan perfectly. There really was because he didn't feel any wings, and besides a lot of people are allergic to feathers and nobody ever sneezes when *you* come around." What can the woman do? She has to admit she's not perfect. She's not an angel. In fact, that's one of her proudest boasts. And she's going to justify her complaints; she's not an angel to put up with everything. But she's caught with her own statement. She has to admit she's at fault in some one regard. Well, let's make it two. "You know, mother, there were two times if you think hard when you were at fault." (Laughter) Let's make it three." But while you're jesting, while you're joking, there's an undercurrent there. And she gets so very, very grateful to you for making it a jesting admission. She's grateful to you for bringing out her lack of perfection humorously. Then all of a sudden, you put *him* on the spot, "And actually, confidentially, your husband hasn't got wings either." Then she accepts that so gladly, but the fact that she accepts it . . .

B: Underlines *her*.

E: Underlines and emphasizes her own lack of perfection. "And you know, I think your child inherits a lot from both of you." (Laughter) "And he does, you know, you're very certain, aren't you?" And we're talking about her defects, and we're talking about her husband's defects, and she starts looking in her child for the defects the child inherited from *her*. She starts looking at her child for the defects inherited from father. But she's admitting defects. Now there's one defense — to burst into tears and say you don't understand. Then you state, "Now I always keep that kleenex handy right there." And she looks over and sees the kleenex right there.

B: And you have understood her.

E: She acts upon it. She reaches over and takes the kleenex. She can't do that without knowing that I understand her. And she goes through the physical behavior of admitting that I understand, and you don't press your point. Then I tell the husband, "All right, now while your wife is drying her tears, suppose you say something." But she has heard, "drying her tears." She's got her orders. She thought I was only talking to her husband. (Laughter) You see, too often the tendency is to look at the woman crying and try to do something in relationship to the woman about her tears. Why not recognize that she *is* crying? And instead of trying to do something about her crying in relationship to her, as the crying object, her husband's in the room; why not do something about her crying in relationship to her husband? "So while your wife is drying her tears, I would like to have you ... " You're doing something about the wife's crying. But it isn't recognized as something being done about her crying. But it is. You started telling her, "I *try* to understand you, that's why I keep the kleenex right there." She has to reach the conclusion that I understand. Just the other day when a woman started crying, I said, "Now you know why I keep that kleenex right there." And she said, "You know, I was beginning to think that maybe I was the only woman that ever cried, and when you said that I knew that they all do, or you wouldn't have the kleenex there."

H: Well, what you keep recommending against is ever stepping one-down or being defensive.

E: No, never be defensive, unless you can use it. (Laughter)

H: Well it's a problem how—it's a task enough to handle one person without getting in a defensive position, but to handle three is more complicated. The only time in this family I'm seeing—the only time the wife ever admitted that she did something that harmed somebody was when I suggested to her that she didn't really understand her husband, and that she didn't mean to do what she did. At that point she said, "That's not so, last time I was here I was being deliberately vicious to him." That's the first time she acknowledged being vicious, but she could only do this when I said she wasn't, you know? You can catch them sometimes;

if they have to contradict everybody, you can trap them in a contradictory impasse.

E: And you know the answer to it, "That's not true, I was deliberately vicious the last time that we were here." My answer would be, "I hope that you will be as free and easy to recognize that next week."

H: Never stop building?

E: That's right. And then if she said, "But I'm not going to be vicious next week," I'd say, "No, why should you be? But I wonder if you, next week, will be as free and easy to recognize that last time you were deliberately vicious. Because, you know, we forget things from one week to the next, and I wonder if you'll forget that next week?" So you've made your sally, and if she accepts the fact that she may be vicious next week, fine, that's okay. If she wants to dispute it, you're still talking about the freedom of recognition and applying it to last week, so you haven't lost any ground. But you're asking her to recognize deliberate viciousness next week, and so you're still building.

H: I don't know how you set these up, Milton, so that you don't lose any ground no matter what they do. It's as if you anticipate answers and give what would be appropriate no matter what answer they give.

E: Yes. But you try and understand the answer that they give. Now, let's see, Frank Bacon played in that play called *Lightning*, wasn't that it? Does anybody remember that? Frank Bacon, an old-time actor. The thing that he taught me was when he said, "No." He was supposed to say, "No," as one of his lines in the play. Frank Bacon ran away with the play because on one occasion he said, "No," 15 times in succession with a different inflection. He just held his audience absolutely spellbound with those different ways of saying, "No." One right after another. One "No" meaning a "startled yes," another meaning a "pleased yes," another meaning a "startled no." It was just simply incredible what he could do with that one word, "No." And he achieved national fame on that "No." That was the time I got the idea that you ought to study words and find out what they mean.

H: They mean, "No." (Laughs)

E: You ought to know.

H: Did you take some training from him?

E: I think you ought to go listen to a tape recording, or take some typewritten material, and wonder what all the different meanings are in that sentence. How would you say it this way? How would you say it that way? The same words.

H: This is relevant to something I was wondering about; suppose we had a family or a couple, and we wanted to approach them in your style, which is different from other styles. Now, what would be the most practical way of learning your style? We have a lot on tape; we've had a lot of discussions.

E: I think one of the nicest ways is entertaining little children. By telling them stories, "Little Bambi flapped his ears? Then flew high?" "No, that wasn't *Bambi*, that was Dumbo."

H: You're not clear enough to me yet.

E: Do you know the story of Dumbo?

H: Yes.

E: He flapped his ears and he flew high, isn't that right? So you call him Bambi, it sounds like Dumbo, a little bit. (Laughter) The child is eager to correct you. But you put the doubt into "flapped his ears." The child wants to assure you he did too flap his ears, but the child can't tell you that because it wasn't Bambi. (Laughter) Do you see?

H: So what do they do?

E: You correct it yourself. "Oh, that was Dumbo." And you bounce the child, and bounce the child, and bounce the child in another direction. The child thinks that you tell the most wonderful stories in the world. (Laughter) Because you stimulated that child and kept that child on edge the whole time.

H: I've done that with just changing names, but I've never done it with putting the emphasis somewhere else so they couldn't quite handle changing their name.

E: How do you deal with a child who says, "I'm not going to eat my meat"?

W: Well, I haven't had to deal with it yet. Our child is a very good eater up to this point.

E: You've got lots of surprises ahead. (Laughter) You accuse the child of being a bird. Then you get the child all involved in proving to you that he's not a bird. Part of the proof that he's not a bird is eating. (Laughter)

B: And if the child says, "Cock-a-doodle-do!"?

E: If he falls in line with that, you point out that he's wearing feathers. He knows darn well he's not wearing feathers at all.

B: At some point he has to turn and prove that he's not a bird, even if he plays along the first round.

E: That's right. The first round, and the second, third round he'll still prove it. And then, when the child tries out with you all of these things, then you pose the impossible for him. He agrees that cloth is feathers, and his hair is feathers, and the eyes are at the side of his head, and this is really a bill and that's what he's eating with, and these are wings with feathers. So you lead him out and he is smugger and smugger and smugger because he's agreeing with you completely. After he's agreed with you completely, you tell him you hope he'll stay awhile before he flies away. (Laughter) Now he's got to backtrack. But you tell him that very simply. Now *you're* following along with him, and he isn't following along with you. Because he's got to backtrack right then and there.

H: I have an idea that you can almost diagram a couple. You see the husband, you see the wife. This is the situation. This is the relationship. This is what it needs. And this is the maneuver that will get them into the situation that they should be in.

E: Well, you know the phrase, the sentence, "The teacher says the principal is a fool." "The teacher," says the principal, "is a fool." And you listen to what somebody says and then you repunctuate it for them. They have to repeat it. You've used their words. They know you heard them correctly, but you didn't hear them correctly because you didn't say the teacher comma says the principal comma is the fool. So you've got them on the alert because you throw in that punctuation, you change the meaning of their words. Then you make honest mistakes like Bambi for Dumbo. See anything that scrambles a meaning. Do you remember Jane East on the radio? The way she could scramble things? "But bald heads are scarcer than hens' teeth." Just what does that mean? (Laughter) And you pause and pause and pause, trying to figure that one out.

W: That's another of these things that deals with just what your patients are bringing you, too.

E: That's right.

W: They make more honest mistakes than anybody I ever heard.

E: I know they do. And you try to be so politely correct. The antagonistic patient says you are a damn fool. And what happens to them when I say, "Well, I know that but I didn't know you knew it." (Laughter) What can you do?

H: This is the willingness to take the one-down position?

E: But you aren't one-down you know?

H: One-downness requires defensiveness.

E: One-downness requires defensiveness. Right then and there they regard you as a very worthy opponent, and it's much better than an hourlong explanation. They've had the carpet yanked out from under their feet. They feel themselves sprawled out, utterly helpless, and completely at your mercy, but they can't accuse you of attacking them.

H: There's just something so tricky about the way you take what a patient is already doing and urge them to continue to do it, and then suddenly it's something different.

E: Well, just take that, "You're a damn fool." "I knew that but I didn't know you knew it." Well, what becomes of that accusation, "You're a damn fool"?

H: I don't know what has become of it.

E: It's no longer an accusation, is it? It's an utterance on their part that puts me in a superior, one-up position. The words are the same. The meaning is the same *but* . . .

H: It turns into a compliment to their understanding.

E: It's a compliment to their understanding, but it puts me one-up on them.

W: They can't stand the compliment, if it is a person who comes in and gratuitously attacks you.

B: Suppose they say, "I knew it, and I knew your wife knew it, but I didn't know you knew it."

E: I can think of a paranoid patient who walked into my office and said, "Is that your wife out in the other room?" And I said, "Yes." He said, "She's the most stupid-looking woman I've ever seen." I said, "You really ought to see her on Saturday." (Laughter) I could have said, "What do you mean? Well, some of that isn't important, why are *you* here?"

W: Well, you find over and over again that with schizophrenics, those parents are pretty concerned about talking with each other, but they're tremendously concerned about talking in the presence of the patient about nearly all of the things that we think are important in the situation.

patient about nearly all of the things that we think are important in the situation.

E: Yes.

W: Then when they haven't talked, when the family is together, they sort of seize us by the arm and say, "Can we talk to you just a minute?" Then they want to bring out everything that they haven't said, or I'm not sure they really do, but . . .

E: They've got a need to talk, but . . .

W: They're terribly afraid to talk in the presence of the patient.

E: I tell them, "You're going to be hesitant about talking in front of the patient, and I think you ought to be, but your reason for talking to me is because you feel very strongly that there are a lot of things the patient doesn't understand. It's the things that you feel he doesn't understand that you want to talk to me about. And you may be right that he doesn't understand those things. But if you talk to me in his presence, and you're really talking to me, and he's not participating, he'll have a chance to listen to what you say to me and perhaps get a better understanding of those things." Then I turn to the patient, "You know you haven't got a corner on all the misunderstanding. There's a lot of things I don't understand. A lot of things your father doesn't understand, your mother doesn't understand, a lot of things *you* don't understand. And we can be charitable and allow the other person to be mistaken, and I think it should be decidedly interesting to you to listen to what your father has to say, to what your mother has to say, and perhaps now and then you can wonder how they can be so wrong on one or two or even three points." So I've given them permission to *wonder*. You know, when you start wondering, you're getting objective. One or two or three points. They're going to make a hundred.

W: It's something that's made a little safe to start with but it can go on from there.

E: Yes. And if there's only one or two or three points that are wrong, that means 97 points are right. But you aren't emphasizing the 97 points. (Laughter)

B: Our general theory, I should say, in terms of what you've been saying, is that what these people do to each other could be described as looking at all the alternative ways of interpreting somebody's need for privacy, for example. Or for somebody's blush, or whatever it may be, and of that spectrum selecting that particular interpretation, which will be pathogenic in that particular situation. This is, on the whole, how they seem to make psychotics of each other.

W: They look over the possibilities and pick out the worst.

B: They look over the possibilities and figure out the most destructive.

E: I go over the possibilities and pick out a nice one.

W: I think this is a good idea, but it seems hard to develop it.

B: Yes, but now how are we going to influence, or teach, them to look over the possibilities and pick out a nice one instead of picking out a son of a bitch. This is the thing they need to know more than any other single thing, I think.

E: The way you teach them . . . I can think of this very, very rigid old maid who came to see me — tense, horribly self-conscious. She developed a terrific abdominal rumble. And she started to blush and squirm, and she was obviously ready to run home and never come back to me again. Then I said, "Did you know that the medical term for that sound is 'botulismness'?" And she looked at me so surprised. I said, "Botulismness is a hard one to spell." What had I done with that abdominal rumble of hers? I had identified it as something that was scientifically named, and furthermore it was a difficult medical name. Hard to spell. Her blushes and her squirms disappeared, and later in the interview, another rumble, and she said, "Is that . . . what do you call it?" (Laughter) I said "Botulismness."

B: I see that you can take somebody's message and put a beneficial frame on it, or whatever you want to call it . . .

E: Her tendency was to take that abdominal rumble and label it fearful, embarrassing, stressing, shameful, humiliating.

B: Etcetera. Yes. And you then substitute it.

E: And I said, "Here's a scientific fact."

B: Yes.

E: With a scientific name. She's had another scientific fact, namely, it's hard to spell, like other scientific names.

W: Well, you see, I find they are cooperating so busily with each other in looking for *bad* interpretations.

B: In the opposite direction. Yes.

E: And too many therapists are cooperating with them.

H: Well it's this kind of a situation, Milton, they all behave as if there is going to be disaster, no matter what they do. They each behave like they feel always in the wrong.

E: Yes.

H: And sometimes they'll say that. Mr. B. will say, "I wish my wife wouldn't act as if I'm going to do the wrong thing no matter what I do." She's learning to drive, he suggests she drive home, she says, "My God, I can't drive out on that highway," and she doesn't assume that he's going to take her on a quiet country road. That's the example they came up with. But they always feel like the other one is thinking that anything they're going to do is wrong. Now, how do you accept this and turn it around?

E: In the situation, or in the explanation?

H: Both.

W: We need all we can get.

E: I think that if I had a couple in the office, and he said she said exactly that, I would say, "You know the surprising thing about it all is this, you're both completely wrong. Your husband thinks you're going to drive home. You think you can't drive home by that road, and that's what both of you honestly believe. I say you're both wrong, and I need your cooperation because I would like to be *right*. So since you live at 23401 Pasadena Road, I would like to have you drive on the Freeway until you can turn at right angles and drive *nearly* home, and then make your husband drive *home*. I'd put her on a different road for a different goal, not too far away from her home. Then she could make her husband drive the remaining couple blocks. Do you see?

H: I see, but I don't see why.

E: I don't want her to refuse to drive home because it's *that* road. I'm going to put her on another road. I'm going to give her another goal. And I'm going to make her husband do something.

H: How does this help with them on the problem of both being wrong, I mean, indicating to each other that the other is wrong?

E: They both prove that the other is wrong. I help both of them prove that the other is wrong. She's not going to drive home; he is. And she's wrong in saying that she's not going to drive; she is.

H: I get it that they both prove they're wrong. Now how does this solve the problem of always feeling that they're being put in the wrong?

E: But you see they have that feeling that they're always in the wrong in an involuntary fashion; you're doing it in a controlled fashion. You want control over that situation. It's utterly imperative. And anything that you can do to build up the control.

H: So once you get them in the wrong, or putting each other in the wrong, under your control, then what?

E: Then you see being in the wrong isn't such a devastating experience. They willingly, gladly, walk into the wrong situation. It's not humiliating. It's being voluntarily done. So she drives out the wrong street. She drives out Camelback instead of Indian School. He drives from Camelback to Indian School. She's made him drive *home*, but she has abided by his wish that *she drive*. It's a voluntary thing. They're both cooperating with me so *I* won't be wrong. There's no sense in all three of us being wrong. So they're cooperating with me. If they cooperate in this regard, I'm going to get them to cooperate in this regard for these other steps.

H: Let's take the B family. Now I see them pretty regularly and typically in the sessions father says something that puts him in the wrong. Mother points out that he's not what he ought to be. Now in taking control of this, would you suggest to them that sometime during this half-hour he's to say something that will put him in the wrong?

E: He says he's in the wrong?

H: No, he says something that puts him in the wrong, or he does something that shows that he's in the wrong. Mother points out that he's in the wrong.

W: Mother labels it.

H: How badly he does, and then he gets silent and defensive about it. But usually something comes up. He says the wrong thing or he does the wrong thing, or he mentions something that he did that was wrong, so that mother can attack him.

E: Very, very often when that happens, I do a repeat on it. Because I missed part of what he said, and I missed part of what she said. So I make him repeat what he said that put him in the wrong. I make her repeat what she said when she attacked him. Thus, it be-

comes something under my control, but not notice-
ably so. Because I missed something that he said. I
missed some of the implications in what she said. So
I'm making him attack himself, and I'm making her
attack him, all over again. I can think of the time that
Lance was teasing Allan unbearably. Allan was about
seven years old. Great big 5 foot 7 Lance was teasing little Allan. And Allan kept saying, "I'll sock you,
I'll sock you." And he was furious, and Lance was
laughing at him. So I went out and said, "Lance,
you're 5 feet 7. Allan doesn't even come up to your
shoulders, he's just a little boy, and look at the age
difference. You're ten years older than Allan. You are
17 and Allan is 7. Allan wants to sock you. And you
wouldn't fight with somebody smaller than you. You
really wouldn't. So kneel down, try to bend at the
same height as Allan. And Allan, just as soon as
Lance kneels down, I want you to walk all the way
around him, look him over carefully, and see *where*
you're going to hit him." Lance kneeled, full of utter
bitter resentment, and glared at Allan. Allan walked
around, and I said, "Well, maybe you better walk
around again, because you might see a better place
to hit him. Just keep walking around until you pick
out the very best spot to hit him." So finally Allan
says, "Right there." I said, "All right, make a fist in
your hand and draw it back, now place your feet so
that you are properly braced. Now move your hand
this way, just to make certain it moves right, and are
you sure you know how hard you want to hit him?"
Lance set his jaw and glared. I said, "All right, now
hit him." And here's Lance's jaw. At the last fraction
of a second, Allan pulled his punch. I said, "Did you
hit him hard enough?" Allan said, "Yes." I said, "Are
you sure you don't want to hit him again?" "No." I
said, "You wait a while, maybe you think you will.

Maybe you better think it over. Hold back the fist and think it over." Allan said, "I don't think I'll hit him again. I hit him hard enough." Lance was looking at Allan looking at me; a grin showed up on his face, then Lance stood up and said, "Well, Dad, I guess I learned something that time." Because we do that sort of thing. Lance was furious, Allan was furious, I set it up. When you have the wife attack the husband in repetition, you're setting it up. You're setting him up, and you're setting her up; punches are likely to be pulled. If not in the actual words, in the venom that accompanies them. And anything that you can do to alter that situation. I was utterly deadly serious with Lance and with Allan. And they knew it.

B: You did not indicate the outcome?

E: I didn't indicate it.

B: There were no overtones to suggest the outcome?

E: No overtones. That's why Lance remained angry until after the punch. That's why Allan remained angry until he pulled his punch. And then didn't really know that he pulled it. (Laughter) And people do behave that way. It's very, very seldom when you ask kids to fight it out seriously that they ever give that full punch. If they ever do give that full punch, you can point out that maybe they ought to punch on the *other* side of the face. The child who really got punched looks forward with dread and horror, and then with such a contrast of feeling of satisfaction and pleasure; that takes all the sting out of this one—this one is pulled.

B: Then you're prepared to go on.

E: That's right.

B: I mean whether it's Allan or Lance, if Allan is hit the first time you would put him through the second time.

E: I'd put him through the second time, but he would have to pull his punch.

B: Sooner or later.

E: If not the first time, the second time. Almost an absolute certainty the third time. But the probability is the first time. Once in a while you get the first punch, and pulling not until the second, and very, very rarely does it happen that they have to pull it on the third try.

B: What it takes is the guts to be willing to go on. And to know that *you* are willing to go on.

E: Yes.

B: Yes.

H: Well, can you explain *why* that punch is pulled?

E: Why? "Mama, can I go to visit Johnny? Mama, can I go to visit Johnny? Mama, can I go to visit Johnny?" "Yes." An hour later. "Why haven't you gone to go to visit Johnny?" "Oh, I just wanted to know if I could." You know that. He was just discovering the range of possibilities. And in this matter of hitting and striking, Allan was so furious at Lance, and he was so helpless. Lance was so much bigger. And he did want to know if he *could* hit Lance. Lance was so much bigger, so much stronger, did he dare to hit Lance? He wanted to know the range of activity. "Mama, can I go to visit Johnny?" Just inquiring to find out if he has that privilege. Allan asked me the other night, "Dad, may I have the car?" "What do you want it for?" "To go to a dance." "How long do you want to keep it?" "Well, first I want to know if I can have the car." I said, "Yes, you may have the car." "May I keep it until midnight?" I said, "Yes." He said, "Fine, I'll be home at nine." I'd asked the wrong questions. Allan wanted to find out the range. And he wanted to find it out by *his* questions, not by *my* questions. He wanted to ask me if he could keep it till midnight. I asked him how long he wanted to keep it. He tipped his hand. He wanted to keep it until nine o'clock. He wanted to know if he had the range up to midnight.

H: There's something in this Lance and Allan business, though, about the fact that you're directing it. You're saying that this is spontaneous, but everybody is arranged by you. It must have something to do with taking it out of their hands, so that even if Allan hit him, it wouldn't be the same sort of hit.

E: That's right, and how would Lance react to it afterwards? Lance felt very guilty about having teased Allan so much. He went all out for a while in entertaining Allan in a pleasing way. Lance is wonderful when it comes to entertaining kids. So he was able to take his guilt reaction out by entertaining Allan. Not because I'd ordered him to, but because he was at liberty to do as he wished. He was at liberty to be furious at me. I didn't seem to care. He could glare at me and glare at Allan, while Allan stalked him so nastily. With your quarreling patients you set them up for each other. You take the sting out of it for them. But you take it out in relationship to doing the things to each other that would actually meet your approval. Lance didn't know that he was really pleasing me. But I do know that Allan, after Lance left the house, felt constrained in some way to tell me how good Lance had been to him. And Lance hadn't asked him to do that. Allan had his own little guilt reactions too, and expressed them.

CHAPTER 4

On Disturbing and
Instrumentalizing

1959. Present were Milton H. Erickson, Jay Haley, and John Weakland.

H: When you see a child and you think the parents need to be brought in, how do you solve the problem that all of us face of getting the parents in without blaming them for the child's difficulties? When the mere fact of calling them in implies that what's the matter with the child is them?

E: I say, "I know you've done everything that you could think of to help the child. But considering the individuality of your child as a unique personality, no matter how fertile your thinking was, it just hasn't worked, has it?

H: So you approve their motivation and imply some inadequacy on what they've been able to think of doing?

E: I approve of their motivation, and I stress the extensiveness of their effort. I leave it an inexplicable question why it didn't work.

W: You also make a point of the value of the child by stressing the individuality.

E: That's right. Then if I think they're going to interfere, I say, "So since we know that all those approaches don't really help, it's going to be my responsibility to see if I can't be as comprehensive in my efforts as you were, but from a different angle." It's a different angle that's going to bring the cure. I'm merely going to be as comprehensive as they were. This matter of face-saving is so awfully important.

W: Yes. It's important enough with couples, but I think it gets even sharper with parents.

E: Yes.

W: They just feel like their whole value somehow stands or falls on that child.

H: Well, do you very often bring parents and child together as a group and have them deal with each other?

E: Not very often.

H: One of the things we see, and I'm sure you see, although you have this approach about the uniqueness of individuals, is we see that typically a disturbed child, whether delinquent, schizophrenic, or whatever, is functioning in some sense — his disturbance is part of the relationship between his parents. That he's somehow in the middle. From this point of view we wonder if you set out, if you were a pair of parents and you set out to create a disturbed child, what would you do?

E: You do the thing that they don't expect you to do.

H: Who is "they" in this? The child?

E: Yes. What do you do if you want to disturb a child? You do the unexpected. You do the wrong thing. You act out of your role. I can think of that 12-year-old psychopathic child at the Worcester State Hospital. Oh me, she would plead with the nurse to buy her some candy, and the nurse would, and oh how beautifully Ruth could smile, and thank that nurse in the prettiest fashion while she delivered a stinging kick on the nurse's shin. She could hug the nurse so gratefully and verbalize a tremendous gratitude, as she ripped the nurse's blouse.

H: What has this to do with the unexpected? The reversal of it?

E: Yes. The superintendent finally was forced to put that 12-year-old Ruth into a seclusion room. Then he called me in frantic haste. He said, "It's Ruth, she has done $400 worth of damage already on that ward. Now she's in the seclusion room, and she's taking the plaster off the wall. She's wrecked the bed and we got that out, but she's still doing damage." "How much damage are you willing to settle for?" He said he was looking over the record. Last year it was somewhere around $5,000 worth of damage she did. I said, "Well, suppose that I see to it she does $400 or $500 dollars more of damage. Are you willing to accept that in place of a higher bill?" He said, "Anything." I walked up to the ward, into the seclusion room, and I said to Ruth, "Now listen, Ruth, that is about the most inefficient job I ever saw of ripping plaster off the wall. Now here is what you need to do. You can break those laths. You can take your dress and you can tear it into strips, and you break those laths, and you can literally make a very nice hammer. Then you can tie a couple of laths together, and then you can use that hammer made out of laths to drive the laths through the wall and that will rip the plaster off the wall on the other side." And Ruth said, "But doctor . . ." I said, "You do that later, here's something else we can do. Do you see that radiator over there?" I said, 'Well, if you jerk it enough times, you can break the pipe, but it's going to take a long time to do it. Now shut up and sit down on the floor with me. We'll both brace our feet against the wall, and we'll take all that, and we'll pull it loose. Come on, sit down." Ruth sat down and I helped her tear that radiator loose by twisting the pipe. Ruth burst into tears, and she said, "You're a doctor, you shouldn't do things like that." I said, "You wanted it done. I helped you do it. Now I'm busy. Goodbye." I walked to the ward. She cried for hours.

H: That's how you disturb a child, by doing the unexpected?

E: Yes. Whenever Ruth got upset, emotionally disturbed, all the nurses would do is say, "Shall we call up Dr. Erickson?" "No." But when Ruth was gay and happy, she would ask the nurse, "Could you call Dr. Erickson to see if he's got time to visit with me?" Ruth wanted me as a friend, but she didn't want me when she was disturbed.

H: Well, you as father, or you as mother, could do the unexpected, but what could you do between mother and father that would disturb the child?

E: I haven't done much thinking in that regard.

H: Gee, we stumped Milton.

E: I don't like the question in the first place.

H: I know that you don't think in this way.

E: I can think of a recent parallel of that. In Atlanta, Georgia, the hotel was very shoddy in their handling of seminars in hypnosis. They promised us nice rooms and everything. After we got there, it was a miserable mess. I went down on a free hour to the hotel restaurant. I was hungry, and I was tired, and I wanted a rare steak. I explained to the hostess and the waitress that I wanted a steak that was seared. You lay it on a hot griddle and then you turn it over. That's all, just seared. If the cook is unwilling to do that, bring it to me raw. The waitress spoke up and said, "I know exactly what you want, my husband likes his steaks that way, and I'll be delighted." I said that if the steak isn't served that way, I'm not paying the regulation price. The waitress brought me my steak, well done. I only had a brief time in which to eat. She said, "I hope this will be all right, sir." I called the hostess over, and I said, "You know, the waitress is very, very sweet and very, very pleasant. She's filled my glass of water. I'm going to tip her, and I'm going to be perfectly willing to recommend to my friends who want well done steaks to come in and have this waitress serve them. But I explained to you I had a brief time in which to eat. I told you how I wanted my steak cooked. It wasn't done. The caloric value of this meat is excellent, but it lacks the satisfaction I'm buying according to the price on the menu. You expect me to pay my bill. I'd like to see my bill, I want to write something on it. I'd like to have the waitress take it and show it to the chef who cooked the steak." The hostess tried to argue me out of it. The waitress took the bill in and showed it. Five dollars and fifty cents was the price of the steak dinner. I reduced the price to $3.00. Then I said, "Now charge it to my room." I said, "You can take it up with the manager." I walked out. They took it up with the manager. The waitress was wary, and she said, "What will happen to me?" And I said, "Don't worry, nothing will happen to you. The manager of the restaurant and the manager of the hotel are really going to come to grief." The next day I went down. The manager of the restaurant put in a great big beef to the manager of the hotel. The manager of the hotel put in a great big beef to the manager of the restaurant. The waitress was very happy about the entire thing. The chef was merely regarded as a hurried, bad boy, but you really aren't going to rebuke him. I went down to see the manager of the hotel. First I got my bill for my room from the cashier. I took it in and showed it to him. They had finally decided to disregard me. A thorough investigation had been made and the customer was wrong. So I went in to the manager of the hotel, the final authority. I said, "Do you agree that a thorough investigation was made?" He said, "Yes." I said, "You're sure it was thorough?" "Absolutely." I said, "Well, what was his report of my statements? Or was the investigation so unthorough that the major party was omitted from the investigation?" He said, "I will okay the deduction." (Laughs) I went back to the hostess. I said, "How did the big shots get along?" She said, "Oh, they had a terrible time." There I had two authority figures fighting. By having the child and the older child. The younger child does something right, the older child didn't, but the blame somehow or another got on to the mother and father, right?

H: That's an example of how the *child* can disturb the parents.

E: Yes. Without the child getting blamed.

H: What about the other way around? Well, we see it in this way, that we think families with a schizophrenic in them, that when the patient begins to improve and behave in a more normal and sensible, self-assertive way, something happens to the parents. One of them either develops a symptom of some kind, or they threaten divorce, or separation; there's a crisis of some kind when a patient improves. Now this seems to us to imply that the patient's pathology has a function in the family.

E: I think you're wrong in the statement that a patient begins to improve, a crisis develops in the family.

H: What's wrong about it?

E: It's this. Mother gets a bad cold or a headache, or father meets with an accident. What I think they do is they take some little thing that frequently occurs in the family ordinarily, and then they seize upon that and psychologically turn it into a crisis. They use something.

H: We haven't had that experience. One example is father went to bed with a heart attack when the patient took a job. He's never had a heart attack in his life, and ac-

tually this wasn't a heart attack. He went to bed because something was wrong with his heart. He'd never
had this before. In another family, the girl – well, it's
complicated – but she had her baby in another state,
and she was a helpless schizophrenic. She decided to
go get her baby. Against her mother's protest she flew
back, got her baby, she brought it home. That weekend mother and father had a fight, and father was im-
potent for the first time in their marriage. Twenty-
three years or so. Now these things keep happening
enough so that there's some concern, or some evidence,
that there is something out of the ordinary with the
parents.

E: Yes, but father has had a little impotence, but it has
never bothered him, or dismayed him, but this is one
time he can really enlarge it to distract his attention
from the other tension.

H: You assume that it's something that has been going on
but is now emphasized.

E: Emphasized, enlarged. Rather than worrying about,
well I'm getting to the heart attack age, now here's
a good time to exaggerate and emphasize it. He's too
busy thinking about that to consider son's improvement. The first thing that I would do in those situations, whenever I encounter it, I disparage the situation. Here's one of fairly long-standing, and naturally
with energy being used up by the problems of read-
justments and acceptance of son's improvements, he
hasn't got enough energy to handle this old trouble
of his.

H: Well, where do you go from here?

E: It may bother him a little bit until the son's improvement is an old thing.

H: Now what we're still on, and still having some difficulty
with, is whether or not you think there *is* some function of a child in a miserable marriage. Whether the

child is used in this marriage for ways that are unfortunate for the child.

E: You always point out to parents that the child has a tremendously important function for them. That they're really not going to get that full measure of satisfaction out of the child to which they are entitled unless the child is happy. That the mother isn't going to get her full measure of satisfaction that she's entitled to out of the child, unless the father gets the full measure of satisfaction to which *he's* entitled. Neither of them are going to get that full measure unless the child gets his full measure of satisfaction out of each of his parents. That if it's a female child, she desperately needs to learn something about the male from her father, because she has to start her learning in the home. You learn to talk in the home. You learn to creep in the home. You learn to walk in the home. You learn to recognize father and mother and other people in the home. In fact, the home is the beginning place of *all* learning. Intellectual learning, social learning, mechanical learning, whatever kind of learning you can think of. So the little girl has to learn everything possible from her father if she is going to grow up in a world where there are men. Where there are males. So you justify the little girl getting something from her father; in fact, you make it imperative that she get something from her father. But she also has to grow up in a world where there are women. Therefore, she better get something from her mother, too. You make it absolutely obligatory on a biological basis that she get something from *both* parents. Then you point out that eventually the little girl, accordingly, is going to be a parent. When do you learn to read a book? For example, a book such as *Gone With the Wind*. You will learn to read in kindergarten, first, and second and third grade. Because you've got to learn the fun-

damental processes of reading *then*. You can't wait
until you're 21 to learn to read; it's too late. So you
learn the fundamental processes. How does one learn
the ABC's of parenthood? After the minister says, "I
now pronounce you man and wife," or after the doctor says, "It's a baby"? Then you've got to deal with
the baby as a totality. You've got no time to learn the
basic things that you need to learn from your parents
when you were a little child. So the parents are obligated to teach their child something about parenthood. So the child will be basically qualified for parenthood when the doctors say, "It's a baby." The
parents can recognize the logic of that.

H: They can often recognize the logic of these things without being able to do them. I mean, I'm seeing a family where I'm sure the mother recognizes the logic of
the daughter's getting something from her father, but
let father and daughter begin to get something from
each other and mother becomes upset.

E: I know, and what do you want to impress upon the
parents? "I think you ought to be awfully sure that
your wife teaches your daughter those feminine things
that your daughter has to learn from a female, from
her mother. And I think that you ought to feel obligated, just as your wife feels obligated, I think you
ought to feel obligated to see to it that your daughter
has that opportunity." Obligated to see that *daughter*
has the opportunity means you're obligated to let
mother go ahead. The parents that came to me, "I
don't think my husband should be the only one that
takes Johnny to the store. I think I ought to take
Johnny to the store and show him how to shop." Father
said, "I'm working, I have very little opportunity. I
like to shop. I think it's nice if I teach my son how to
shop. His mother has him all day, why should she take
that one privilege away from me?" I asked the father,

"Well, tell me how do you shop at a supermarket?" Then I said, "All right, now how would you shop in a corner grocery store?" He said, "The procedure is entirely different." I said, "That's right. Now tell me, do you think you shop in the supermarket exactly the same way your wife does?" He said, "No, she probably has a different procedure." "Do you think your son ought to learn how to shop in a corner grocery store?" "Well, of course, but the procedure is entirely different." "He isn't going to do very much shopping in the corner grocery, but do you think he ought to know that procedure, even though it's different?" "I certainly do." "Do you think he ought to know the slightly different procedure your wife has shopping?" I put up the same argument with the wife. Then they finally agreed. Then my question was, "What are Johnny's rights?" They said, "What do you mean?" I said, "Both of you have dictatorially been saying, 'I will take Johnny shopping.' I think that's wrong. I think Johnny's got some rights. I think Johnny ought to say, 'I'm going to take father shopping, or I'm going to take mother shopping, or I'm going to take you both shopping.'" Now there's a petty little quarrel brought in for me to arbitrate. It could have grown into a tremendous analogism.

H: Well, one of the things you do is — you have the oddest way of taking at face value what the quarrel is, while at the same time assuming it's more than that. I mean, apparently if somebody did come in with just that as the quarrel, it would obviously represent problems in the family of some severity. The father would feel that mother was using child and shoving him out in some way, that he was feeling left out.

E: Yes, but in the practice of medicine — there is an old farmer who hasn't had a physical examination or medical checkup for years and years. He thinks maybe there's something wrong with his heart. That's a horrifying idea to him. He isn't ready to face it. And what does he do to the country doctor? He goes in and says, "You know, Doc, I've been working awful hard in the field lately and I guess I'm getting some kind of arthritis in my feet, and would you mind looking at them?" The doctor better do that. The doctor who examines those feet with the greatest of care notices that the veins are quite prominant on the dorsal of the foot. Then he wants to check up on the veins in the legs. You see where it goes? And he can wind up with the conclusion that the veins are really all right. The farmer knows he's had a complete examination. Then the farmer says, "Well, what's the bad news?" But if the doctor suggested that he'd better have a complete physical examination, he would say, "I'll go to some doctor who knows what I'm talking about. I said it's my feet."

W: So the smart doctor has to pay attention to the feet, and yet be damn sure to know enough not to stop there.

E: That's right. But you don't say, "You need a complete physical examination." You just don't.

W: Let's try it a little different way. One of the things we were really trying to bring up was not just a matter of what do you do about it, but in what way you see children as getting caught up if there are difficulties between the parents that they can't handle. How do the children get involved when the parents are having trouble with each other?

E: The tendency of the parents to try to instrumentalize their children. There is such a wealth of ways in which they instrumentalize their children. There's a beautiful joke: The lady of the house answers the doorbell. Just as she is about to speak to the salesman who had rung the doorbell, another salesman comes up. The lady of the house speaks to the second, "Just a moment if you please, I'll get rid of you just as soon as I get rid of this other salesman."

W: How is the connection of that with the parents and children?

E: There is the situation in which something's got to be done about this. Instead of meeting the salesman's needs, the salesman is utilized as an instrument. "You stand here while I get rid of this salesman; then I get rid of you." "Sonny, you stand there while I get rid of your dad; then I'll get rid of you." Only it's done unpleasantly then. This joke was done sweetly. The second salesman is obligated to stand there. The first salesman is obligated to await being gotten rid of because the second man is standing there waiting for him to be gotten rid of. It's a very binding situation.

W: Yes.

E: They're both caught in it. And the father was gotten rid of while a child is made to wait, then I'll get rid of you.

H: About the only thing you can say is, "No, get rid of me first."

E: Yes, but you can't do that. Neither salesman can say that. He doesn't want to be gotten rid of.

H: Yes. How do you keep the parents, or help the parents keep the child, from manipulating them?

E: I asked some parents . . . I saw only a mother recently. Do you know how long it takes their 11-year-old boy to tie his shoestrings? Twenty-three minutes. He helped his mother set the table. It took him three-quarters of an hour. "Oh, I'm busy. I'm hurrying." In three-quarters of an hour he got one plate on. His mother said, "I timed him. His father and I have talked it over. Shall we call you in or should we continue to try our own method? Jimmy's only started this recently. Now what do you think we ought to do?" Well, this is the answer, should they call me in. It's a doctor and his wife. I said, "Why don't you approve of Jimmy's dawdling? Every one of my kids has learned of the absolute peril of dawdling. I can outdawdle anybody, while hurrying as fast as I can. You dawdle, you use the child's pattern. You raise the question of something the child is expecting, something he wants. You start to get it, and the child is waiting very eagerly, and something distracts you. You apologize abjectly to the child, "I'm hurrying just as fast as I can but I've got to get this first." The child waits, and you get that done, and then you start. You start a conversation with someone and it drags on, and on, and on.

H: The child will connect this with his dawdling?

E: I can think of one medical student who dawdled horribly. I had given a final deadline. That book review, all book reviews, had to be in by 8 o'clock on Saturday morning or there would be flunks. I said it had to be given to me in person, and that any that weren't handed to me in person would not be accepted. Oh yes, that dawdler showed up out at Elouise. At the last minute, exactly 8 o'clock. I had seen him headed for my office. So I tipped someone off to buzz me on the phone, and I walked up to the office and I said, "Well, the phone is ringing, excuse me," and I said on the phone, "Good heavens, really?" And I rushed out. The poor sap waited. Do you know, it was noon before I got back. (Laughs) He sat there, because when he had waited five minutes, he had committed himself to waiting ten minutes. You see?

W: Oh, I know that's the position you get in once you begin to wait.

E: You've committed yourself to waiting.

W: Did you accept him as having got there; that is, you accepted his report when you came back finally?

E: Yes. At noon he was literally raging. I walked in with

a friend and said, "I'm happy." He said, "I'm not, and you certainly fixed me." I said, "Your grade on your book review is 'A' because you learned an awful lot of insight." (Laughter)

*   *   *

H: Well, what do you do about the way one parent makes an attempt to draw a line and the other sabotages. Father decided he's had enough of this child doing this sort of thing, but as soon as he starts to step in and do something, mother steps in on *him*, or vice versa.

E: I ask the child to use his intelligence in watching the sabotage of the parents. I've had children aid in correcting the parental sabotage because mother hates to have the child point out to her, father hates to have the child point out, "Your behavior is not really pure."

H: We'll have to tell Gregory that one for his family. It's just so explicit in that family that every time that father tries to chastise that boy in any way – it's the boy in that film you saw – mother is on him like a shot. Very typically, these are mothers who protest that father never takes responsibility for the children. That's one of the reasons we begin to see a system going on.

E: Oh, there's one thing I want to emphasize to you. I think it's awfully important in every growing family for the children to be aware of the fact that parents can disagree and that they ought to approve of quarrels between parents. Because the kids ought to learn on their own how to have difficulties with their siblings and surmount those quarrels. They ought to learn that parents can surmount quarrels. That teaches them that they can take issue with the parent and, win or lose, still surmount that. It's so false that so many parents try to teach a child, "We have always painstakingly concealed from our children the fact that we have differences." My statement is, "Don't you want your children to think you're human? Don't you think they ought to know you're human? Don't you think they ought to know that you can quarrel and still love each other? Don't you think they ought to have a realistic view of life?" I've had parents look at me in abject horror at what they had done, and say, "Now, how can we quarrel in front of the children?" "Take issue on a very, very minor point. It'll shock the poor kids. But don't stage a big quarrel."

CHAPTER 5

Ordeals of Children and Parents

1961. Present were Milton H. Erickson, Jay Haley, and John Weakland.

E: In dealing with a mother and boy, I can think of little Johnny, 12 years old, who wet the bed every night. He was utterly hostile towards his mother in that regard. After sizing up the situation, I told Johnny that I had a remedy for him that *he* wouldn't like. It would be effectual, absolutely helpful, absolutely certain, which he wouldn't like, but which his *mother* would *dislike* more. (Laughter) Now, what could Johnny do? If his mother would dislike it more than he, that would be fine. He could put up with anything that made his mother suffer more. Then my proposal to Johnny was rather simple. I pointed out to Johnny that his mother could get up at 4 or 5 a.m. in the morning, and if his bed was wet, then she could rouse him. He would then get up and sit down at a desk and copy so many pages from any book he chose, putting in from 4 to 7 o'clock or from 5 to 7 o'clock in the morning copying material. His mother would watch him do that, watch him learning to improve his script. To Johnny it sounded horrible, getting up at 4 or 5 in the morning. Mother had to get up first. Sounded horrible, having mother sitting there, watching him *improve* his script. His handwriting was really terrible.

So Johnny found himself in the situation of making
his mother watch him improve his script. He only had
to do that on mornings when his bed was wet. Nothing more disagreeable than getting up at that hour
of the morning to improve your handwriting. (Laughter) So it wasn't long before Johnny, instead of a wet
bed every morning, he began skipping mornings.
Pretty soon he was having only two wet beds a week,
then a wet bed every ten days. Mother still had to
get up.

H: Every night and check?

E: Every morning and check. Finally it was once a month,
and then Johnny reoriented himself entirely. He developed the first friendships he had. It was during the
summer. Kids came over to play with him; he went
over to play with kids. His marks in school that following September were greatly improved. He was
even elected Class President — the first real achievement. Now that's playing mother against son, playing
son against mother. It's that same thing of, "I've got
the remedy for you; you won't like it." Then digress
to the fact that mother will hate it even more. He
wants me to come back to, "What is it?" and he's all
for it.

H: Mother's all for it too?

E: Mother's all for it too: Improvement in handwriting becomes *the* primary goal. The dry bed becomes an in-
cidental, more or less accepted thing. It's no longer
the dominant, threatening issue at hand.

H: Mother can hardly not go along with that since it's for
her son's sake; to help him and all.

E: And the whole family relationship is improved. I had
one interview with the father to size him up. The
father was a loud-voiced man who walked into this office, sat down, and spoke as if I were about 60 feet
away from him. He asked me if I didn't know that all

kids wet the bed until they got about to age 16, that's what he did, that's what his father did, he was very certain I had done it. He was certain every other boy grew up that way, and what's this nonsense about curing his son of wetting the bed?

W: How did you respond to that?

E: Oh, I let father explain to me. (Laughter) He enjoyed the interview, and he shook hands with me, said he was delighted to have such an intelligent listener. When the son and mother came in the next time, the woman said, "My husband said that he had explained things to you." I said, "Yes, that's right. He explained at very considerable length." Her facial expression said, "I know." The son had a pained look on his face. My statement was, "So far as I'm concerned, I'm going to forget about everything that was said. You don't have to, but then of course you weren't here, you only have some ideas of what he said. I'm just going to forget them, because it's the ideas that you and I and your mother have that are important. It's the ideas that you and I have, and Johnny has, that are important." You see what that does? It's tying myself to Johnny first, then tying it the other way around. Having me allied first with Johnny, then having mother allied with me. You see, Johnny's going to stand by me. Because I'm going to forget what his father said, and Johnny would like to forget that. Then I tied mother to me by having her join me in forgetting what father said.

H: And this shuts father out of the picture pretty well.

E: Shuts father out of the picture, puts him off on a side track there. But it's not a hostile putting him aside.

W: You've already heard him out.

E: I've heard him out, and they know it, and father's come home and told them. I'm just forgetting about it. No particular anger or distress.

H: Why wouldn't you include father in your instructions about it?

E: How do you mean?

H: I mean, you confine it to an activity with mother and child only.

E: Because of the father's absolute opinions. He knows *everything*. During the discussion of how all boys wet the bed until they're about 16, he also pointed out to me that any man who had even a particle of common sense would vote for his certain political party. The father has his opinions.

H: What do you suppose his response was to the boy stopping wetting the bed?

E: It was very complimentary. He told the boy, "Well, you learned to have a dry bed faster than I did. Must be you're a lot smarter than I am."

H: (Laughs) That sounds extraordinary.

E: And that was the end of that.

W: It seems to me in that if you let him express his opinion, then somehow this is satisfactory enough to him so that he can accept the actual change.

E: He had told *me* off completely. He had implied that my political sense was deficient. He had already told me that my psychiatric sense was deficient.

W: So it's done.

E: Then he could afford to be very generous. Besides, it wasn't the psychiatrist that did it for his son. It was the superior brain power he bequeathed to his son. He was the boy's father and therefore . . .

W: "My boy did it!"

E: "My boy did it."

W: Now, on the bed wetting, would you assume that the bed wetting was a product of the relationship with mother? It was something they had worked out together?

E: The father was so cruel and harsh and cold and matter-of-fact. He yelled at his kids. No words of sympathy, nothing at all. His accusations to his wife that she was babying the brats too much, "Every normal kid's got to fall and hurt himself and yell awhile. That's what I did when I was a kid." Those were the things that the father said. When the little boy would try to go to his father, he'd get shoved aside, "I'm busy, I've worked hard all day today." Then the mother tried to make up for it. The boy's fundamental reaction was, "I want love from my father. He doesn't give it. Mother always steps in and makes it unnecessary for him to give it." Now the father's statements ever since the boy could remember, "Every kid wets the bed, it wouldn't be normal if he didn't. I wet the bed." Of course, the mother got awfully fed up with those wet beds.

W: Didn't you, in fact, reverse that picture somewhat? Didn't you arrange things so that the mother, of course for his own good, which again is appropriate, was giving the boy a rather hard time all these mornings, and father was in a position where he could then identify the boy with himself and be pleased with something he was accomplishing.

E: The boy is giving the mother a hard time.

W: And the mother is giving the boy a hard time, in a way.

E: Yes, but somehow or other that added up to his improvement, so it was a joint achievement, a satisfactory relationship that was really approved and blessed by the father, wherein he did get recognition and acceptance from the father.

H: That's the first one of these sort of punishment deals which involves two people getting up in the middle of the night, or morning.

E: I used that procedure in quite a number of my cases.

H: Where you get two up?

E: Yes.

W: Oh my, Jay has got half the population of Palo Alto up in the early morning now. (Laugh) He's going to have the other half up shortly.

H: Quite a few people, including local psychiatrists, are trying this now. It's effective. But I've never tried getting two up. Could you give some examples?

E: You see, mother, in watching her son's handwriting improve, was really satisfying a craving, a need, to see excellence in her son. Her son could take a great deal of pride in his improved handwriting. It was a joint venture with shared pride and shared satisfaction. When the two would bring the handwriting to show me, it was just an eager boy, an eager mother, showing me this beautiful handwriting. I could go through it, page after page, and point out this letter "n," that letter "g," this letter "t," and discuss the beauty of the script.

W: The thought that has come to my mind here is that maybe the only thing that some people can share initially is an ordeal.

E: An ordeal, that's right.

W: People that can't share pleasure may be able to share an ordeal and then move on from that to something else.

E: Well, did you see that movie of the chain gang where the white man and the negro are chained together, and they escaped.

W: I read about it, I didn't set it.

E: I didn't see it either; Betty did. The white man hated the colored man, and they went through one ordeal after another, being welded closer and closer into an understanding, brother relationship. Betty said you could literally see it growing. But then it has always been in human history when you fight through a difficult thing with someone else, it welds you to the other person. You've shared a very vital thing. Since

Johnny has a dry bed, his father has played ball with him, come home early from the office.

W: It would be important to have this ordeal one where they would get somewhere together as a result of it.

E: Yes. And usually you want the ordeal to lead to visible, attainable results. I can think of, let's use the name Johnny all the time, Johnny had been picking at a small sore, a pimple on his forehead. He had picked at it for two years so that it was a continuous ulcer. His father had resorted to all manner of punishment. So had his mother. So had his school teachers. Little Johnny was picked on by his classmates, his schoolmates. He had been told all about cancer. Johnny explained he just could not control the impulse to pick at it. His father had broken his bow and arrow. I don't know how many toys the father deprived him of. Then finally the father brought him in to me. The first interview I spent with Johnny was defining ownership. I picked out the bow and arrow right away to begin with. Whose was it? The father admitted it was Johnny's. How was it Johnny's? It had been given to him for a birthday present; therefore it was his. In what way should an ulcer be treated? Bandaids, salve, medication of various sorts, yes? How would you use a bow and arrow to treat it? How would breaking a bow and arrow be treatment for this ulcer? The father was very embarrassed, and the son was eyeing his father with narrowed eyes. So the father flushed and squirmed quite a bit. I asked Johnny, who was about 12 years old, if he did not think that he could honestly credit father with at least good intentions, despite the stupid behavior. (Laughter) You see, both of them had to accept that.

W: Yes.

E: So Johnny could call his father's behavior stupid. He could also credit him with being well-intentioned, best-intentioned. Then my next question was, "How much further ought we to discuss the medicines that don't work? Or can we forget about all the medicines that don't work? You've had it for two years, all the medicines from the broken bow and arrow to a selling of your bicycle. Those are medicines that didn't work. What shall we do?" Johnny's idea was that I should take charge. I told him, "You won't like the way I take charge, because I'm going to do something that will clear up the ulcer. You won't like one bit of it, all you'll like is when the ulcer is healed. That you'll really like." I said, "I found out that your spelling is poor. Your spelling is poor because when you write a word, you're very likely to leave out letters." I'd verified that. Because always you check on their school work to see what's there. Johnny left out letters when he wrote words. So I pointed out to him that every weekend was to be devoted to Johnny's curing his ulcer on his forehead. Father was to do the weekend chores for him. It was a rather triumphant glance that Johnny gave me and his father. So I inquired about all weekend chores – I'd ask the mother privately about them. Well, Johnny was supposed to mow the lawn; he was supposed to do weeding in the flowers. He did quite a bit of watering. There were numerous little chores. Clean up the dog tags on the lawn. Everything that you would expect of a small boy with quite a good-sized lawn. There was a garden in the back. So we went over all of those chores. I wanted to know who inspected the lawn when Johnny did it. The father did that. I said. "Well, in between working on your ulcer, because you can't work on it steadily, in between the times when you're working on your ulcer, curing it, Saturday you go out and inspect to see how well your father is handling your chores. I think you ought to start on Saturday morning on your ulcer about 6:00.

You know you'll take things much more seriously when you get up that early in the morning to do it, because it *is* serious business." Now, what I'm demonstrating here to you is the slow and aggravating, dragging out, shaggy dog technique of presenting the therapeutic plan. Because, what happens to your patient: He just leans forward, wishing you'd come to the point of the whole thing. (Laughter)

W: "For God's sake, tell me what it is you want me to do, and let's get it done."

E: That's right. He's much more interested in finding out what on earth it *is*. He's crediting you with being thoughtful, deliberate in your presentation, he knows you're not trying to rush things over on him, and so he's waiting eagerly for you to come to the point. Well, the point with Johnny was essentially this; I was showing him a few little side issues, "You write with a pen, you write with a pencil, some leads are colored, but ordinary pencil lead would be all right. Ordinary pen and ink or ballpoint pen would be all right." (Laughter) We've got that out of the way. "I suppose ruled paper would be better, and I think your father can get ruled paper so wide. I think probably about that wide would be the best. Now, this is what I think you ought to do starting at 6 o'clock. Of course, if it's only five minutes to six, you might as well start then instead of waiting until 6 o'clock. Or, if it's five minutes after six, what's the difference, five minutes." (Laughter) Then you break the news to him. "This is the sentence I think you ought to write, 'I do not think it is a good idea to pick at that sore on my forehead.' 'I do not think it is a good idea to pick at that sore on my forehead.' Now write it slowly, write it neatly, write it carefully. Count each line when you've got it done."

H: Why did you have him write, "I do not *think* it is a good idea..."

E: That's what he asked me, "Why don't you have me write 'I *can* stop...'?" See? Let *him* put in that correction. Now how do I know that he would put in that correction? "I do not think.." is extra words. If he can only cut down the length of that sentence. He pointed that out to me. He said, "I'd love to write, 'It is not a good idea...'." He wished it were shortened, and so he's emphasizing, "It is not a good idea."

H: I see.

E: So I told him to count each line when he had it done. "Always check each line because you wouldn't want to leave out a single letter. You don't want to leave out any of the little processes, or the parts of healing, that take place in an ulcer like that." I had the most tremendous stack of sheets of ruled paper containing that sentence. Written with pride and enjoyment. He took a coffee break, which was essentially a fruit juice or water break, every two hours. I'd explained to him he'd have an aching hand on the first forenoon. What ought he to do about that? I pointed out to him at each fruit juice break he should do this sort of thing: open and shut his hand rapidly to relax the muscles. I told him that would increase the fatigue, but it would keep the muscles limber. Johnny wrote on that every weekend, Saturday and Sunday; his father didn't have to urge him at all. The father said, "I knew what I had to do; I did the most beautiful job you could ever imagine on that lawn." Johnny took such pleasure in discovering a leaf on the lawn. He really got the lawn fixed up thoroughly, the garden fixed up thoroughly, the garden fence repaired. All the odd chores done, and Johnny wrote his sentences. In a month's time the ulcer was healed. A year later there's been no recurrence. What did Johnny show me a year later? "There's my stack of paper. Any time I pick on that, I'm going to write another sentence." Now, that chronic, indolent, horrible ulcer – you literally can't see the scar. It's a beautiful case of healing. Now he had had his head taped. His family doctor had bandaged his head. Everything was done to prevent the boy from touching that. But he'd slide his finger up under the adhesive tape. What did I do with that handwriting? I drew his attention to the fact that he did have a bad habit of dropping letters out of words. I took his compulsive picking away to a compulsive writing accurately in which he could take a wholesome pride.

W: Did you do anything in particular about how they would wind up this when and as the ulcer healed? Or did you just leave that as something they would work out?

E: I had told him that I didn't know how long it would take the ulcer to heal. It was my feeling, since he had had it continuously for two years, that it really ought to take a month. That he could watch it from every three, four days to the next three or four days in the mirror to see how it's progressing. Not day by day. He would be able to find out when it was healed; then he might want to write an extra weekend after it was healed.

H: How many hours a day did he write on Saturday and Sunday?

E: He took his breaks. He started at 6 o'clock. I told his mother to be sure to be very dilatory in preparing his breakfast. (Laughter) So that he'd get a rest there. Then he'd write for another hour, take his coffee break, inspect his father's work, come back and write. My feeling was that after dinner time he should really be free of the day's work. In fact, I really didn't care if he quit at four.

H: That was very nice of you.

E: You see, you make the matter of quitting time a matter of indifference to *you*. It takes away the punitive aspect.

H: Yes. Now this was another situation where you used two people; I gather you didn't include the mother in this set of instructions, except for the breakfast.

E: Well, the mother had protested the breaking the bow and arrow. She had protested the selling of the bicycle. I've forgotten what other things. So she was on the boy's side. But the boy's resentment for the breaking of his bow and arrow – that was his property, it was a birthday present to him. You see, it was taken as the repository for *all* the resentments; and it was the father who did it.

H: You wouldn't assume here that a big problem in it would be the conflict between mother and father about this problem. That the perpetuation of the problem had something to do with the conflict between mother and father.

E: I didn't even think about that. The primary question was how to get rid of that ulcer on the boy's forehead. How to enlist his aid, enlist his father. I was simple and matter-of-fact in telling father he was stupid. Getting father and son cooperating in acknowledging the father had the best of intentions. Then taking all of that thing and equating it with poor medication, inappropriate medication, mistaken medication.

W: Then by your question, "How long should they go on considering medicines that haven't worked," you really get that all in a bundle and get rid of it.

E: I got rid of that. Why bother with a complete analysis of all the medication that didn't work? Let's go on to something that *will* work. You see, the more he wrote, the more justification he had for inspecting father's work. The more he wrote, the more accurately he'd have to write. All the dice were loaded in favor of progress.

H: Did the father inspect his work to see if he left out any letters?

E: No, that belonged to *me*. That was made clear; that belonged solely to me. If he wanted to show his writing to his parents, that would be all right with me; but I'm the one who wants to see it. I'm the one who'd make comments on it. That father and mother were so utterly astonished at Johnny's absolute pride in his handwriting, and the thousandth writing of that long sentence was beautifully done. I'd put it in his case record and asked him how long I should keep it. Because it would fill my file, which was much too full. How long should I keep it?

H: What did he say?

E: Oh, Johnny said I might like to keep it for a number of months. Then what should I do with it? He said, "It's just waste paper then." I also examined every page. I told Johnny I could take a quick, hasty look at every page. Were there any particular pages that he recalled that I should give more than a fast scrutiny to? Which made him absolve me from minute examination. Now that's maneuvering him, manipulating him. But it gave him the role of an equal, of an earnest participant in seeking a common goal.

H: Now, you said earlier you had talked to the mother about the chores. Did you anticipate that this was what you were going to do?

E: Oh no, I wanted to know something about the whole family situation so that I could hastily look it over and pick out something. You see, you pick out something in the family situation because that gives you the proper framework. The therapy is being accomplished in relationship to something within the home. In relationship to certain values in the home, certain obligations. When Johnny decided that he didn't need to write anymore, he told his father, "You can go back to your work; I'll take over mine."

H: But now, you wouldn't assume that—one of the things

we notice more and more is that the parents have a certain sort of conflict which is about something that's a problem with the child. It can be a whole range of things. But it's almost as if they need him to have a problem to fit the conflict they have with each other. Then they don't deal with what they feel about each other because what they fight about is the kid and how he's being mishandled by one, and so on.

E: Yes.

H: So the kid almost has to produce a symptom in order to keep this system going.

E:Yes, and when you then correct the child, or cure the child, then they've got a new and unfamliar child. Then they have to go back to their own private war between themselves and not include the child He's a stranger now, and a pretty self-sufficient one.

W: This means also, then, that after this the child is in a better position to not get involved in their private wars.

E: Yes. He's learned how to get out of it. Father's been in too close contact with that child ever to want to get in close contact with that child again. (Laughter)

Some years ago my son Allan and my son Robert, four years apart in age, had just reached that age at which each constituted a perfect foil for the other. And Allan would say, "bad boy," to Robert. And Robert would enragedly scream back at him, "I'm not a bad boy!" and the row was on. I put up with it for a while and then I told Robert and Allan that I was fed up with it; that I would teach them not to do that sort of thing when they irritated one another. And just as they picked unexpected times to start the brawling between themselves, to my discomfort, I would pick a totally unexpected time to teach them *not* to. I also told them that my method of teaching would be very effective, that they didn't really like fighting with each other. While they wouldn't like my method of teaching, they would be very glad to learn better than to fight. I reminded them of that several days apart. Robert had scheduled a party for that Sunday afternoon. Allan had scheduled a show that he wanted to go to very much. They were about to leave at the same time. I called them into my office. I said, "You know, I've been promising to teach you not to quarrel. It would be awfully convenient for me right now. I've had so much inconvenience with your quarreling in the past, so I'm going to take this afternoon to teach you not to quarrel. Robert said, "I've got a party," Allan said, "I've got a show." I said, "I know, I'm sorry, but the teaching comes first, and I don't know how fast you can learn." (Laughter) So I took them into the bedroom there. I said, "Now, Robert, in the past when Allan called you a bad boy, you screamed at him, 'I'm not, shut up!' Then Allan said, 'Bad boy,' and you'd scream that at him again. And Allan, you always tell him, 'Bad boy, bad boy'; sometimes you whisper it, and sometimes you say it in a low voice, and sometimes you say it louder. Then you wait for him to scream at you." I said, "All right. It's now one o'clock. The two of you can start. Seems to me it doesn't take many seconds to say, 'Bad boy, bad boy,' seems to me it doesn't take many seconds to say, 'I'm not, shut up!' So I'll be here in the office, you'll be there, and we'll leave the door open so I'll know how thoroughly you're working hard to learn not to say that." At the end of 15 minutes, they said, "Can't we stop now." I said, "You did it awfully slowly; you didn't seem to have much interest in it, and not much spirit. You just said, 'Bad boy, bad boy,' but as if you didn't mean it. Robert just said, tiredly, 'I'm not, shut up,' (Laughter) and he doesn't seem to mean it. Now, I would like some good, spirited honest-to-goodness rowing, and at 2 o'clock I'll tell you whether or not you've done a good job." "But the party!" "But the show!" I said, "I told you before, I didn't know how fast you could learn." They went at it (Laughter) strongly for about five minutes and then they weakened. At four o'clock I said, "Well, you really didn't put on a good performance, but you've been at it long enough, so maybe you have learned. At all events, I'll have a chance this next week to find out how much you've learned."

H: You kept them at it 'til four o'clock?

E: Well certainly. The next day Allan got irritated with Robert and started to say, "Bad..." (Laughter) Burt and Lance went through this same sort of thing. Burt is now 32, Lance is 30. They reminisce and recall some of those situations I put them in. They'll tell you it was a pretty horrible experience because, as Burt and Lance say, "First thing you do, you don't want to say, 'Bad boy,' and you don't want to say 'I'm not, shut up!' You wish you'd never thought of those words ever. And you've got hours to think it over and wish steadily for one hour, two hours, three hours, 'I wish I hadn't said that, I don't want to say that.'" Every repetition is a reinforcement of their feeling, "I don't *ever* want to say that."

* * *

E: Lance, my second son, announced very proudly at the luncheon table one day, "Daddy, do I have to do what you tell me to?" I said, "Within reason." He said, "Do I have to eat dinner?" I said, "You don't have to, but it's a good idea." "Well, you can't make me eat my dinner." I said, "No, that's right. You can eat it." He said, "I'm not going to eat my dinner unless you make me, and you can't make me." I said, "Why bother about the dinner, you've got a glass of milk there. I can make you drink your milk." "You can't make me drink my milk." I said, "Oh, yes I can." I said, "Go ahead and eat your dinner because we don't need to think about dinner, let's think about milk." So he ate his dinner and said, "Make me drink my milk." I said, "I will." "You can't make me." "Oh, yes I can." And we kept up that interchange: "You can't." "I can." "You can't." "I can." I said, "I can make you do anything I want you to do." "You can't, you can't even make me drink this milk." "You've got to do exactly what I say." "I don't." "You have to do exactly what I say. You have to drink your milk because I'm going to say. 'Drink your milk.'" "I don't have to do what you say, I won't drink my milk." I said, "You have to do what I say," and I followed that and the broken record turned around and around on that for a while. And I suddenly came up with, "You have to do what I say." "I don't." "You have to, don't drink your milk!" He looked at me in a startled fashion. I said, "Drink your milk," he had to put it down. "Don't drink it, drink it, don't drink it." He had to do what I said, but he had to defy. I said, "Spill your milk." He couldn't solve it by spilling his milk. "Put the glass on the table and leave it there." He didn't have to. There he was caught. He couldn't spill it, he couldn't drop it, he couldn't put it down on the table. A horrible bind. "Don't drink it, drink it."

W: What was the outcome?

E: After a while he said, "Daddy, I'm in a fix. Let's quit," Yes, last time he was here he recalled the incident, and he said, "I hope you've worked that swindle of yours on the other kids because it really teaches you a lot."

*   *   *

E: You treat the medical student who wants to be impudent. He'll make some impudent remark to you, and you tell him rather simply, "I really don't know if it took much courage to say that. I think you have enough courage to repeat it." He's hooked. He's got to repeat it, or he's got to admit he hasn't got enough courage to say it. If he says it again, he feels silly. "All right, you had courage enough to say it a second time; I wonder if you've got courage enough to say it a third time." (Laughter) If he says it a third time, he's hooked again. He wonders how on earth to get out of that. (Laughter) He starts wishing right then and there he had never, never said anything like that to you. You're using the class as part of your background. Now he knows you're using the class. It's a miserable situation, and all he's doing is wishing and wishing, and he's totally lost. I've had attendants, nurses, even doctors at Wayne County General Hospital become angry enough to be willing to lose their job, and they'd come into my office and really cuss me out. After that happened a few times the word went around. Then only when new employees came, the old employees would try to get the new employee (Laughter) to come in and tell me off. They would even prime the victim with what to say to me. I don't know how well you know hospital attendants, the way they can lose their temper and things they can say. But they would come in and give me a complete resume of my character and my antecedents, and perhaps wind up by saying, "You're a G.D. S.O.B." I'd be listening quietly, the whole time, attentively. I'd say, "All right, you've just said I'm a G.D. S.O.B.; you would have been speaking more accurately, don't you think, if you had said I'm a G.D. dirty S.O.B., a bastard. Now really, I think you could have said that. I think it would have expressed your feelings more adequately. You could say I'm a bloody bastard of a son of a bitch. There are a lot of other words you could have put in."

H: This is the accepting bit again.

E: Yes. Where does it leave him? Because you have taken his horrible denunciation of you. You have castrated him in the most helpful, thoughtful, considerate way.

H: It's that mixture of benevolence that does it.

E: It's that mixture of benevolence, or innocence, or simple stupidity, or naiveté that you put into it. Somebody, unfortunately, told Allan, when he was in high school, he gave him a scathing denunciation and told him, "You are the most stupid person I have ever seen." Allan roared, "If you think I'm stupid, you just ought to see my brother!" Allan said it was the funniest thing in the world. This person just stood there and stared stupidly; then he turned in disgust and walked away, completely whipped. Somebody tried to tell Betty Alice that she was terribly stupid. She did it in very nasty, catty fashion. Betty Alice turned to the woman and, in outraged tones, said, "That's because I work at it!" (Laughter) It was the outraged tone that acknowledged that she worked at being stupid, that she wanted *credit* for stupidity. That she demanded it as her absolute right. That the woman wasn't really giving her enough credit. What can the assailant do in that case? You have joined with them, you are agreeing with them, you are pointing out the inadequacy of their attack, you are making them wish they had never attacked you with such an inadequate weapon.

H: I'm sure they do.

E: A father and a son were here. The father's a doctor. The son was a few days from being 21. The son graduated from high school in a class of 112 students. Quite a few of those students came from the other side of the tracks. Father was a doctor, very brilliant man; his wife's a brilliant woman. It's a talented family. There's no question about the son's intelligence. A few quick questions privately with the father told me something about the high school makeup. It's on the borderline where students from the south side of the tracks and the north side of the tracks had attended the same high school. Sonny boy graduated number 112 in that class of 112. I pointed out to the father and the son that I thought the father and mother had been horribly wrong and mistaken in being irritated and displeased by the son's failure. That to graduate at the bottom of his class—in fact, he didn't quite graduate at the bottom of his class because he had to go to summer school in order to complete that one additional hour. But that was well within the range of error, because nobody can judge things absolutely accurately. That the father and mother, instead of blaming their son, should have congratulated him, because it must have taken an awful lot of doing to always get a little bit lower mark than the morons in the class did. That took calculated study, thoughtfulness and very keen judgment—always to come in underneath the morons in the class. The fact that he had to take an extra hour, you couldn't expect him to be always, absolutely accurate on a thing as difficult as that. You should have seen that father's face and that son's face.

H: You said this to the father in the son's presence?

E: I turned to the son, and I said, "Now, don't try to tell me it was *easy*. (Laughter) Always to slide in under the dumbest guy in the class." I said, "Now, after you graduated from summer school that year, you went to the University of 'X' and enrolled. You took the full allotment of cuts from every class, you handed in your work late, you tried always to get a 'D' grade, being careful to avoid a 'C', careful to avoid an 'F'. You knew it would enrage your father and mother if you flunked out. You finally figured out how to make them madder than ever, even though you didn't flunk out. The week of examinations, you left school without permission. You didn't take the exams, so you didn't flunk them, you didn't pass them. Your father and mother still don't know whether you would have passed them or not. Nobody knows. But they can't say you failed them. Your father and mother decided that they would really put you in a bind; your father got you the appointment to Annapolis. You passed the entrance exams with one of the highest scores. There were 1,199 men in your class. That really gave you some competition. (Laughter) You managed to get position 1,169 in a class of 1,199. In 1,199 students, there have to be at least 50 screwballs. But you managed to get position 1,169 in spite of that competition. After that, you forced the Academy to kick you out. After giving you the highest grade on the entrance examination, you forced them to kick you out for complete inaptitude." I said, "That wasn't easy to get. Because you had to go about it in such a careful way. You accidentally left this button unbuttoned. The upperclassmen would call your attention to it and give you a demerit slip. Somehow or other in buttoning that, you loosened your belt, you got your tie crooked. (Laughter) You ran your fingers through your hair but you ran your fingers through the hair the wrong way. You salute by knocking your cap off your head. (Laughter) It took ingenuity, intelligence, and never-failing alertness to get that innumerable list of demerits that added up to complete ineptitude. After you got the highest grade in the entrance exam for that entire class. Then after that you went home and you showed your father and mother that you were not a criminal. You walked into a little parking lot 25 miles from home, wandered around until you saw a car with a key in it. You carefully got the car out of the parking lot, drove 25 miles, while obeying the speed laws very carefully. You parked the car at the top of the hill three blocks away from home, walked home, called the police, and told them there was an abandoned car in front of your house and you wish they'd come and pick it up. You gave them the address. So a stolen car was returned before the owner knew it had been stolen. No laws really violated, except driving a car without permission, safely. And you got a job to prove to your parents that you would work." I said, "Now you're not going to like the next thing I say, you've been smiling smugly, happily, giving delighted glances at your father. You're pleased about my analysis of Annapolis Academy, and you've enjoyed that immensely, but from now on you aren't going to enjoy it. (Laughter) Because all I'm going to do is state the simple truth, and the madder you get, the more you're going to realize that I am speaking the truth. So, get ready to be mad. The thing is this, you got a job, and you thought you'd show your parents how you could be self-supporting, and you met this girl and she was a nice, cheap, easy lay. So you started living with her. You call her your finacée. You've talked to your parents about marrying the girl, and all she is is a cheap, common tart, a whore. You know it, and I know it; and you'll be ready to kill me before you'll be ready to admit it." You should have seen that guy jump up waving his fists, grinding his teeth. He told me, "One more word about my fiancée, one nasty word more, I'll disregard your age, your cane and I'll clobber you." I said, "You mean that if I call that tart that you call your fiancée a whore, you will really clobber me?" (Laughter) And he burst into tears and just burst out of the office. His father said, "Now you've done it." I said, "What do you think I've done?" He said to me, "The boy's going back East, home; he isn't going to go into therapy with you." I said, "Do you want to bet on it?" He said, "I know my boy, he's going to go back home." That's exactly where he did go. He went home, broke off with that goddamned cheap, lousy, good-for-nothing whore, and came back here for therapy. (Laughs)

H: One of the things that has come up several times in this session is your unconcern about antagonizing a patient. It doesn't seem to bother you at all.

E: No, why should it?

H: Well, I just think it would most people.

E: You see, when you antagonize people, they are waiting, looking for action. They're ready to defend themselves. They are so angry they want to hit. Their whole learning has been, "If I hit, I get hit back, so while I'm ready for offense, am I also ready for defense?" So you've got them in that situation. Now in order to be master in the situation, they've got to know, "Is he going to slug me? Is he going to run?" And you sit there very quietly, passively, thoughtfully, verbalizing further insults. Or, a careful, detailed analysis of the situation. They are waiting desperately for you to make some move. You haven't. The longer they wait for a move on your part, the more they're committed to waiting. Do you recognize that?

H: I'm not sure I understand it. I mean I'm not sure I understand why you want them to be committed to waiting.

W: So they'll follow you, I think.

E: They're waiting, waiting for you to give them a lead to follow.

H: The more they wait, the more they're likely to follow the lead.

E: They'll follow the lead. I'll give you the example of the young man who came in here without an appointment one evening. He just walked right in, shut the door, pulled the curtain, sat down in the chair. He said, "You don't know me, but I've come here tonight to mash the hell out of you."

H: This is the man who was going to mangle you. I remember you told us about that. That's the one you handled by defining the situation as one where he could be very successful at that.

E: All I did was, I sat there and got his age, his weight, his height. I pointed out that there'd be no satisfaction in mangling me, messing up my office. I couldn't even put up any kind of struggle.

H: Now, that's a situation where somebody has come in to get you. When you have a husband who's scared to death of his wife, and therefore won't say what's on his mind, and you say to him, "I don't think you have the courage to say what's on your mind," now this is needling the devil out of the guy.

E: If he is too much of a weakling, you temper that. "I don't think you've got the courage to tell me what's on your mind, but I'm very certain it's clear in your own mind." He doesn't like to admit he doesn't have the courage to say it, but he is going to admit to himself that it's clear in his own mind. So he's started some honest-to-goodness thinking.

W: So how you would phrase that might depend on whether you could see he was really at the boiling point, in which case you could make it stronger, or that he was just sort of glum, in which case you'd given him a little more while putting a finger on it.

E: Yes. You want him to function within his own capacities.

H: Now it's a similar situation where you say to the father that what he's been doing has been stupied. This again is risking antagonizing him.

E: Yes.

H: You seem to not mind this a bit. This is not usual with psychiatrists.

E: Yes, I know the average psychiatrist is awfully afraid of antagonizing his patient. I think that in psychiatry, as in medicine, you ought to be perfectly willing to palpate an abdomen and find out where the tender pain is instead of keeping your fingers two feet above the abdomen when you palpate for fear you might hurt the patient. The patient's entitled to know where he hurts. (Laughter) So are you.

H: Well, have you ever lost a patient because you antagonize them that way?

E: I've had them irately go home, and call me up maybe a week later, two weeks later, as long as a year later and say, "May I come back?" The only patients I've ever lost by that were patients I didn't want to keep.

H: On this antagonizing business now, I wonder how routine it is with you, in the sense that I notice in most of your hypnotic inductions, a part of your challenge is to have the subject do something they don't want to do, antagonizing them somewhat.

E: Yes.

H: I wonder if you parallel that in therapy.

E: I've got a nice, episodic schizophrenic. We're at swords' points. I'm making him shovel out an irrigation ditch. I pointed out to him yesterday that he had done fully five minutes' work in an hour-and-a-half's time. My tendency is to berate him. Yesterday he did an hour's work in about three-hours' time. This morning he stopped in here almost livid with rage. He said, "You've got to admit I'm improving." I said, "Yes, I do have to admit that you're improving; so is your work performance, And boy, did that need improvement!" I said his work performance had improved, and he could feel happy about that. And did it need improvement. It did. He had to admit it needed improvement; it did improve. So he's got to admit both things. That it was bad work performance, and I'm giving him credit for improved work performance. That same patient, his mother, in her seventies, took him by the collar at the front door and dragged him in here and said, "I can't stand him any longer." So I shut the door and drew the curtain (over the door) and I said, "Now sit down." She said, "I can't stand it anymore, I can't stand it. I can't put up with him. His moaning and groaning and his saying that he's suffering when he isn't suffering. I can't stand it." I said, "Now listen, mother, will you, for heaven sake, shut up. And Tom, do some deep squats. I know it will hurt your legs, you're not used to them. Do 25 deep squats. Mother, you count them for me." (Laughter) I told her to shut up, be quiet. Then I gave her the privilege of counting the punishments I was inflicting on her son. So when he had done 25 deep squats, I turned to his mother, and I said, "I'm awfully sorry, he's going to have some awfully sore legs. But he's been sitting around too idle, too inactive. Now if he gets a little soreness in his legs this afternoon in that irrigation ditch, it may limber them up a bit. So Tom, get down and do some push-ups. Mother count them." So he did push-ups and deep squats. And deep bends. Mother counted them.

H: Well, what was that about? What were you after with that?

E: Mother couldn't stand it. She was at the end of her patience. Her desire was simply to run back East and abandon her son, which she would regret before she got 200 miles away. She'd come tearing back full of guilt and shame and distress and agony, which wouldn't do her any good, which wouldn't do the patient any good. Her other son, who's a psychiatrist, warned me in a long distance phone call to watch out for mother's sudden mood changes. So I stopped mother from making one of her flights.

W: You found something they could do together.

H: That's right. The patient was quite willing to do the deep squats and all if you told him to?

E: Yes. I don't know why patients do what I tell them to do. (Laughter) This son irritated the life out of his mother by sitting and moaning and groaning. She would much rather go to the library to read and spend the day. So I had her get a library book, drive her son out on the desert, dump him out of the car, and drive three miles down the road. She sat there and read until, ragingly, he completed his walk to the car. The mother objected to it the first day I suggested it to her. I told her, "Now listen, your son is going to fall down, he's going to crawl on his hands and knees, he's going to wait to stir up your sympathy. Take a deserted road in the desert where there will be no passersby. He will try and punish you by making you sit there and wait for five hours, but remember he is out there on the ground for that length of time. He'll get hungry." The son tried everything, but his mother obeyed my instructions. He walked three miles. His mother said, "You know, I'm getting to like this reading out in the open." He walked more and more briskly. He sometimes volunteered to walk. That way he can cut it down to one mile. (Laughter) But he's volunteering, you see. His mother is so astonished at his improvement. His psychiatrist brother said, "Put him in a hospital, there's no hope for him." Mother didn't want to do that, and mother today wanted to know when she could start him bowling. So you see, he *is* improving.

W: Did you give that instruction to the mother alone, or was the son there?

E: In the son's presence. Because I wanted him to know that I knew exactly how he could stumble and fall, and faint, and anything else he wanted to do.

H: How did she get him out of the car?

E: She once picked him up by the nape of the neck and brought him in here. She's a very forceful woman.

H: Apparently. What you are doing is encouraging her to help her son, just as she always has.

E: Yes. But this way, not in that old, soft, maternal way. But in a way that someone else says is good for her son.

W: And not to back out in the middle.

E: That's right.

H: It also involves them both in an ordeal.

E: I can assume that one way for that schizophrenic patient to exercise would be to walk. As sure as I get him started walking, he's going to find some other exercise that's much better, perhaps the bowling that his mother suggested. He very happily gave me his mother's note on bowling today. Well, I don't care whether he walks or whether he bowls, but he's going to get fed up with that walking and do the thing *he* wants to do.

H: Well, you try to establish a class of things for them to do, and then give them one item in that class which they're not going to be very happy to do, and you want them to "spontaneously" find another item in that class.

E: Yes.

CHAPTER 6

Directives and
Joining Children

1961. Present were Milton H. Erickson, Jay Haley, and John Weakland.

E: One of my patients was asking last Saturday, "Why on earth have I ever done all the things you told me to do?" She said, "You never made an issue of it. You just expected it in such a way that I had to do it. When I balked or tried to avoid it, I always wanted you to try to force me. You always stopped short. I'd try a little harder to make you force me to do it." Each time she tried a little harder to force me to do it, she'd come closer to me – to the performance of what I wanted her to do. That psychology that Garrett and John worked on us grade school kids. Garrett in September would meet the school kids and greet us happily and say, "Now kids, as you come past my orchard here, there's lots of apples on the ground. Help yourselves. Eat all you want to. If there's some special big apple up in the tree that you would like, climb up carefully, don't slip and fall or hurt yourself, and take it and eat it. But I think you'll find plenty of apples on the ground." We always helped ourselves to eating apples at Garrett's. John met us and said, "Now listen, you ornery kids, I've got a big, high fence around my orchard. I've got a mean dog in there. If I catch any of you kids, I'll have that dog bite you, and I'll spank you. I want you kids to keep out of my orchard." You know what we did – there was the dog decoy detail that went into the orchard (Laughter), the others picking the apples at this end, stuffing them in our shirts. Those were our ammunition for birds and telephone poles. Garrett's apples we ate. We were very reasonable about Garrett. Poor John.

W: You took a lot of throwing apples.

E: We took a lot of throwing apples. But you see, that's human nature. Whenever you start depriving people of anything, they are going to insist that you give it to them. When I instruct patients to do something, the patients feel I'm ordering them. They want me to be in the unfortunate position of failing there. Therefore, they've got to keep me at the task of ordering them. And when I stop ordering them, at the right moment, then they substitute for me. But they don't recognize that they're substituting for me. For example, this one patient, it used to be that the worst punishment on earth was to take my stethoscope and listen to her heart. In the past it had always given her an acute panic. I would say, "Now listen, stand up, and here's my stethoscope. I want you to come over here and pull your blouse up so I can listen to your heart." Then there was the defiance. And my passive indifference. I didn't seem to be demanding that she take another step. I didn't seem to be putting up any fight at all. So she'd take a tentative step to order me to induce her to move more rapidly (Laughs) toward me. I'd seem to give some semblance that I was about to tell her, "Come on." But I wouldn't quite make it. And she'd wait for me to say, "Come on." The she'd take another step toward me. (Laughs) Then again I'd start as if I was going to order, "Come on." Then she'd have to take another step. Until finally she'd be standing by me. I'd say, "Well, I'm ready with the stethoscope." She was waiting for me to tell her, "Get that blouse up." She'd say, "Well, you want me to pull up my blouse. Well, I'm ready." (Laughs) The need to defy, to resist, to insure the chance that you can defy, that you can resist. And I'd start the situation developing for her to resist. Then she had to develop it. But she always lost. When she would finally pull up her blouse and I'd listen — that triumphant smile on her face. "All right, go ahead and listen." "You've been so slow I've lost my interest." But I told her, "Come over here and lift up your blouse so I can listen." So I can. She's obeyed. She's come over, she's lifted her blouse. So I can listen. That's all I asked in the first place. I didn't promise her I was going to listen. (Laughter) So it's all *her* performance. Every time I pulled some other task on her, it always worked out in that same way. Weasel wording. Exact wording. Literal wording. She had had, let's see, 12 years of depth psychoanalysis. She was the most horrible mess I ever saw. She's a very competent citizen now. I see her about once a month. Just to make certain after that long, long period of disability, that she isn't going to reestablish any of those habits. The diagnosis was hysteria. (Pause) Is this meeting your needs?

H: Yes. We'd like to move it more, as much as possible, to couples or families, but obviously how you handle a patient is related to this anyhow.

E: I can cite the case of a 12-year-old boy who, regardless of what time his parents got him up, wet the bed at 12 o'clock. He would lie and rage at himself until about 2 o'clock. Then he'd get up and simply walk into his parents' bedroom and insist on sleeping between them. They spanked him repeatedly, but he went right back in between them for another spanking, until they gave up. He didn't enjoy sleeping with them, they didn't enjoy it, and they all had broken sleep. I knew the boy wouldn't go on Boy Scout hikes because he wet the bed. I knew his parents had bribed him with pet rabbits, and I knew they had given him a collection of minerals and stones and he liked those. He also had a Boy Scout blanket. So I raised the question of this self-punishment. Regardless of what his parents did he wet the bed and punished himself by lying in bed. Then, not satisfied with that punishment, he got up and went into his parents' bedroom for more punishment, and they gave it to him. Why didn't he take charge of his own punishments and deliberately and honestly and openly administer them to himself? We finally agreed that he should spread his stones out over the concrete floor, draping the Boy Scout blanket over them, go to bed, wet the bed at midnight, awaken and instead of lying in a wet bed say, "Well, I want punishment and I'm going to administer it to myself," and get up and lie down on the blanket on the stones and sleep there the rest of the night. I am not absolutely certain of the length of time, but it was under a month. He gave up his rabbits because they were a bribe to him, kept his stones, and he continued for approximately a month to sleep on the stones after midnight. Finally, he decided that he'd had enough of that, he could sleep in his bed, the way he wanted to with a dry bed, and that was that.

H: And you didn't tell his parents about this suggestion to sleep on the floor? This was between you and him?

E: That was between the boy and myself. I told him that if his mother found him sleeping on the stones, he should tell her that what he was doing was his own arrangement with the psychiatrist, and that she could talk to me but I wouldn't give her any satisfaction.

I had in one of the parents and said, "You want me to take care of this boy? Let me do it my own way. I'll send you a bill *after* the boy stops wetting his bed."

H: Once again you have him do something voluntarily to solve an involuntary problem.

*　　*　　*

E: I had an 11-year-old boy who blocked completely on reading. I questioned him about his father's summer vacation, and I had quite an argument with the kid. "You know L.A. is 750 miles," I said. He said it was not, he had been to L.A. in the car, with his father. He had been to Spokane. I knew that was 350 miles. The kid and I had a horrible argument about it. I proved my point, or tried to, by getting out a map and a ruler and getting the mileage, 200 miles per inch, for 350 miles that made one inch and three-quarters. I started looking for Spokane then, and he started looking elsewhere on the map. He couldn't read the word "cat." I knew Spokane was somewhere near Salt Lake City, he pointed out to me it was near Portland. He read all the names on the map. He said I might be a good doctor, but I sure was stupid about distances. (Laughter)

H: Once he was able to read the names on the map was he able to read other things?

E: "Well, maybe I am stupid on distance, but I can tell you a lot of things about Salt Lake City," and I proceeded to do so. "And tell you a lot of things about L.A.," and I proceeded to do so. "I haven't been to Cheyenne, but I can tell you a lot about that." What's the implication?

H: That he could tell you a lot about the places he had been to?

E: I can tell you a lot about Cheyenne, I haven't been there.

In fact, I don't know anybody who has been there. How did I find out my information?

H: You read it.

E: That's right. He showed me he knew a lot about this city, that city. I never inquired how he got it. All I know is he went into the proper grade. I never did get around to teaching him how to read. I bragged about my membership in AAA. How they send out maps showing all the places of interest. I like those maps; that way I knew what to look for when I am in a certain city. I never mentioned the descriptive material. His father joined the AAA in preparation for that summer trip. An entirely new route was mapped out. The kid read up on all the data on every spot along the trip, and the father obligingly mapped out a route that took him to this and that national park, to see this particular scenic thing, and that particular scenic thing, and the kid did like the trip. Why should I bother with these first grade readers, second grade reader, third grade reader, fourth grade reader? In September, just before school began, I said, "I suppose you will have the same old idiotic argument with your teacher, but she'll lose it." He wanted me to name the appropriate grade, the 7th or the 8th. His teacher knew darn well he belonged in the first grade. She lost the argument. "She really thinks she knows it all. But she is a teacher, and she has to think she knows it all, until someone shows her. She really does have to know it all, that's what she is hired for."

*   *   *

H: Do you ever see a children's problem that can't be resolved without bringing in the parents?

E: You bring in the parents without really bringing them in. That is, the parents called me up and told me about little Johnny, ten years old, who wet the bed every night. They had done everything they could do to stop him. They had shamed him. They had whipped him. They had deprived him. They had enlisted the aid of the schoolteacher. They had enlisted his classmates in grade school. They made him wear a sandwich board saying, "I am a bed wetter." They belonged to a small sectarian church, and they had the entire congregation pray aloud that Johnny quit wetting the bed. They had an eight-year-old brother wear a sign, "I don't wet my bed, but Johnny my older brother does." The parents had gone all out. They gave me this history over the phone. It was pretty horrible. So I told them I'd see Johnny, and so they explained to Johnny that they were taking him to see a nut doctor. In other words, further degradation. They dragged him in to see me. Father had him by one hand, mother had him by the other. Johnny was dragging his feet. They laid him face down on the floor here. I shoved them out of the room and closed the door. Johnny was yelling. He had to pause to catch his breath to yell, so I yelled. He turned to look at me. I said, "It's my turn. Now it's your turn." So he yelled again; I yelled again. We paused for breaths. I said, "It's my turn, not your turn. You know, we can keep right on taking turns, but that can get awfully tiresome. I'd rather take my turn by sitting down in that chair," pointing to this chair. "There's a vacant one over there." So I took my turn sitting down in this chair. Johnny got up and took his turn sitting down on *that* chair. That expectation, you see. I had already established that we were taking turns with that yelling; then I changed the game to taking turns sitting down. Then I said, "You know, your parents ordered me to cure you of bed-wetting. Who do they think they are that they can order *me* around?" In other words, Johnny had had enough punishment from his parents. So I stepped over on Johnny's side of the fence by saying, "Who do they think they are, ordering me around? I'd rather talk to you on a lot of other subjects. Let's just drop this talk about bedwetting. You know it. I know it. They know it." I said, "Now, how should I talk to a 10-year-old boy? You're going to grade school. You've got a nice, compact wrist. Nice compact ankles. You know, I'm a doctor. A doctor is always interested in the way a man is built. You've got a nice, rounded, deep chest. You're not one of these hollow-chested, slump-shouldered people. You have a nice, deep chest that sticks out. I'll wager anything that you're good at running. With your small-sized build, you undoubtedly have got good muscle coordination." I explained coordination. Sports that require skill, not just beef and bone. Not the sort of stuff that any bonehead could play, but the games that would require skill. "What do you play?" "Baseball." "Is there anything else that you do?" "Bow and arrow." I said, "How good are you at archery?" He said, "I'm pretty good." I said, "Well, of course, that requires eye-hand, arm-body co-ordination." So I explained that and emphasized the depth of his chest. It turned out his brother played football. His eight-year-old brother was much larger than he was. "Football is an awfully nice game if you've got just muscle and bone. Very good. Lots of great big, overgrown guys like it." The deprecation of the larger eight-year-old brother in terms of the game. So we talked about that, and I talked about muscle coordination. "You know, when you draw back on your bow string and aim your arrow, what do you suppose the pupil of the eye does? It closes down, tightens up. You see, there are muscles that are flat, muscles that are round. Muscles that are short. Muscles that are long. And there are muscles that are circular.

Like the one at the bottom of your stomach. You know when you eat food, it closes up. The food stays in your stomach until it's all digested. Then when the stomach gets rid of it, the circular muscle opens up at the bottom of your stomach, empties out, closes up, waits for the next meal to digest." A muscle at the bottom of your stomach. Where's the bottom of your stomach when you're a small boy? So we discussed that for an hour. The next Saturday he came in all alone, and we talked some more about sports, and this and that, never mentioning bedwetting. We talked about Boy Scouts and camping. All the things of interest to a small kid. On the fourth interview he came in wearing a great big, wide smile. He said, "You know, my ma has been trying for years to break her habit, but she can't do it." I said, "That's right. Some people can break their habits quickly. Others make great big talk about it and don't do anything about it." Then we drifted on to other topics. About six months later he dropped in socially to see me. He dropped in when he entered into high school, socially. He's now in college. "Ma's been trying for years to break her habit. She can't break *her* habit."

W: Did you find out what ma's habit was?

E: Cigarette smoking.

W: She couldn't break her cigarette habit even though she got the whole congregation to pray for that boy? (Laughter)

E: Now all I did was talk about the circular muscle at the bottom of the stomach closing up, holding contents until we want to empty it out. Symbolic language, of course. But all that beautiful build-up about eye, hand, arm, body coordination, the praising of his chest, the praising of his wrists, ankles. Apologizing because I'm a doctor and I notice that sort of thing. I didn't even advise the parents to let their son alone. He was my patient. I took my turn, he took his. I took mine, he took his. And I took mine and he took his, to get him in a chair.

W: Well, was there any opposite to that? Is there anywhere you feel that it would be absolutely essential to have some sort of direct dealing with the parents?

E: Oh yes. I can think of another bedwetting case where I told the parents, "Absolutely don't you dare go in your son's room. Don't you make the bed. Don't you change the linen. Don't do anything. Don't say anything. I'm handling it." So the parents really kept out of it completely in that sort of a fashion. Sometimes in the bedwetting, you tell the child, "Now listen, you can't disappoint your parents *all* the time. They know darn well that you are going to wet the bed. That's what they honestly believe, and nothing is going to change their minds. They're going to hint that to you over and over and over again. Now listen, it isn't a pleasing thing to ask of you, but it's a necessary thing. Now let's see, today is the third of December. Oh, I suppose, why not pick on December 13th. That'd be a good day. The thirteenth is considered an unlucky number. So on the night of the thirteenth, just go ahead and wet the bed. Even if you have to try pretty hard to do it, but wet it. Don't disappoint your parents. They know darn well you're going to do it, but you don't have to do it *every* night. So you pick the night you do it." As sure as he picks the night, he is saying, "I have control." But he doesn't know that. So he comes and tells you how hard it was to wet the bed deliberately. I tell him, "Well, it was worth it for your mother's sake. Now, the thirteenth. I suppose we could wait until the 13th of February, or January, or March, June or March." You see, that juggling back and forth, but you may have two deliberate bedwettings, sometimes even three, but you hold, primarily, in reserve, that suggestion for February and January. You backed up, you see. June, March, you've gone way ahead, you've backed up. March is way ahead of February. You're making progress.

H: How do you determine which one to use with which kid? Is it possible to say at all?

E: Well, it's the reflection of the personality as you talk to the child. A mother came in to tell me she wanted me to take care of her son. She said, "He's a liar, he's a cheat, he governs the house by throwing temper tantrums, and he's got the sharpest tongue imaginable." So the mother was very, very bitter. She said his father was a sexual pervert. "I don't know all the perverted activities his father engages in . Once in a while he comes to bed with me, but he's got a lot of solitary perversions. He uses clothes, *my* clothes, for his perversions. I think he dresses up in my clothes. I think he masturbates. I think he ejaculates on my clothes because I have to take them to the cleaners. So there's not much relationship between the boy and his father. The father is short-tempered. He screams at the boy, and the boy is unwilling to come in to see you. I told him I was going to bring him in forcibly if I had to." She said, "I don't know if you can handle him. I've taken him to other doctors, and he just threw temper tantrums, and they would not have anything to do with him." So she brought him in. This very charming, sweet-faced soft-voiced boy. He said, "I suppose mother's told you everything about me." I said, "She's told me some of the things she knows, but not everything about you, because there are a lot of things about you that only *you* know. And she couldn't tell me a solitary one of those. I'm wondering if you're going to tell me any of those things?" He said, "I might not." I said, "I know that. But let's settle one thing right away. I'd rather sit here and waste my time doing nothing with you than sit here and watch you having a temper tantrum on the floor. So what shall it be? Temper tantrum on the floor? Or shall we sit here and waste time, or shall we get down to business?" He said, "Not that way. We can waste time. We can get down to business. And I can still have my temper tantrums." He was keen, wasn't he? He's never had a temper tantrum. I've had him very violently angry, especially when he threw mud balls and water bombs at the neighbor's house. I asked him to describe exactly how he felt, what pride and joy and happiness and triumph he felt when he smashed that water bomb. And the mud balls on the neighbor's house. That infuriated him. I said, "You're willing to have a temper tantrum here. You never have, of course. Here's a beautiful chance! Now what are you going to do, have a temper tantrum or tell me?" He told me how angry he was. His mother says that he is tremendously improved. That he now has friends in school, and he is popular there, well-adjusted and well-behaved at home. That's what the boy says too. He laughs with a great deal of amusement over his previous behavior. All I saw of the mother was periodically when she would drop in on her way home from work to hand me a check. She soon got tired of that and started sending the check by the boy. His willingness to recognize that he could waste time, work with me, or have a temper tantrum. See, whatever a patient offers you, I think you should be willing to accept, without being disturbed.

H: Well, have you ever had . . . has it been a long time since you had a patient manage to disturb you in the office?

E: Oh no.

H: How does that happen to you?

E: There was a 12-year-old boy. I knew his grandfather. I knew his grandmother. I knew his father. I knew his mother. I knew his stepmother. One morning he came downstairs, and the stepmother was there, and the baby was in one of these little chairs. He had a bicycle chain in his hand, and he said to his stepmother, "I want to see you dance." She said, "Are you joking?" He said, "Oh no. See the baby? Start dancing." He made her dance on the kitchen floor for one hour. His father brought him to me. I never saw a more utterly vicious child. Until finally I told him, "You know, I don't like you, and you don't like me, and you're deliberately speaking in intonations that even get under *my* skin. So I'm going to ask your father to pick you up and take you home and take you to another psychiatrist." I wanted to beat that kid no end! His intonation was marvelous for irritating people. It was a work of art that he pulled on me, and the guy knew he was pulling it on me. It was the most incredibly beautiful, artistic job imaginable. My feeling was that a kid of that age, keeping his stepmother dancing — I've seen the grandfather, and the grandmother, and the father, and the mother, and the stepmother, all as patients. I knew their personalities. But here's an utterly, completely vicious boy. The father did ask me, please, see him again. I found out that the father was awfully unaware of the criminality of that kid: petty thievery, torture killing of cats, torture killing of puppies.

Another patient bothered me no end. So I asked him to go and see some other psychiatrist. He came in and, taking his history, I found he liked wandering the desert on horseback, and then I found out why. He had stolen several hundred pounds of dynamite, and he had made booby traps out in the desert. Periodically he'd go for a ride on the desert to see if he got a cow, a coyote, a rabbit, a person. He was always hoping to get a person. That horribly smug, pleased, happy way in which he told me about it. The intonation said, "I know you don't like it, I know you hate it, but I'm top dog." I don't like those patients. I saw too many of them in prison.

H: There's something else about families that I have been thinking of as you talked. I think you make a differentiation between the world of children and the world of adults, such as they are incompatible worlds. I gather that when you work with kids, you make this differentiation sharper for them, and with the parents.

E: Have you ever thought of a small child's point of view? When my daughter, Betty Alice, was here last September, she took Roxy, Margie and Christy for a ride in the car. The little girls were sitting in the back seat having a little-girl conversation, and one of them happened to ask a question. The little girls were debating what the answer was, and Betty Alice volunteered the answer, quite unthinkingly. Deep silence. Then Christy spoke up rather clearly to the other two little girls and said, "See, it's just like I told you. She's just like a mother: listen, listen, listen." (Laughter) So when you consider how the poor little kids are stuck with these adults who listen, listen, listen. And Betty Alice said she felt so horribly ashamed and so *outside* of the little girls' world.

H: She hasn't been out of it very long.

E: No, she's only 23. It's such a clear statement.

H: Well, when you work with parents and kids, you work to get this differentiation more clear for *them*?

E: Oh yes. You're perfectly willing to let the kid know that you're an adult, but you let the child know that you have at least an honest *desire* to understand his world. Oh yes, Johnny was a very, very brilliant seven-year-old boy. One spring he decided that he would demonstrate his omnipotence. Mother was divorced. Mother is a school-teacher. Johnny had a sister a year older than he. Sister is well-behaved. One day at school Johnny defied the teacher. I think Johnny's brighter than that teacher was. Johnny did a good job. And Johnny decided to defy the whole school. Then to defy the neighborhood. His mother when she brought him in to me said, "He's a hell-raiser. I've got no authority, nothing at all, the last straw was reached the other night when in the middle of the night Johnny got up and took a metal ashtray and battered a hole in the wall, knocking plaster off and the laths off. Johnny says he's going to show me that he's going to be the toughest hoodlum in Arizona." And Johnny said, "That's right. And an old man like you can't do anything at all about it. My mother can't." So I said, "Well, you really mean that? You think you can win?" Johnny said, "Yes, I can." I said, "Then you're not afraid of what your mother will do, are you?" Johnny said he wasn't the least bit afraid of what mother did. I said, "Well, you're not afraid to have me give your mother advice?" "Give her all the advice you want." So I asked Johnny when the tug-of-war should occur. I said, "Today is Friday, tomorrow is Saturday. That would be a really good day to take your mother to the cleaners if you can." He said, "I can, and I will." So I talked to the mother. The next morning mother awakened him and said, "Let's wait until after breakfast. I'd like you to have a good breakfast." Johnny threw the eggs on the floor and said, "I want bacon." Mother prepared the bacon. He threw some more stuff on the floor. The mother let him get a good breakfast. Then mother picked up a glass of water, a couple of oranges, a couple of bananas, and put them on the bookshelf right along side their telephone. Johnny wondered about that. Mother went to the bathroom. Mother weighs 160 pounds. Johnny was age seven. Mother came back from the bathroom. All of a sudden Johnny found himself flat on the floor, mother sitting on top of him. Beside the telephone. Johnny yelled, "Get up off me." Mother said, "I haven't finished thinking things out yet." Johnny kicked and struggled, but it was 160 pounds on a seven-year-old. After about an hour, Johnny said, "I'll be good." Mother said, "Are you sure?" Johnny said, "Yes." Mother said, "I have not yet learned how to believe you." Johnny raged and kicked and yelled obscenities and profanities. He tried to get out from under that 160 pounds of weight and couldn't. (Laughs) So after a while he sobbed and said, "I'll be good." Mother said, "You know, you told me that before, and then you kicked up a worse fuss than ever. So I have not yet learned how to believe you." Johnny said, "I'm thirsty." Mother said, "Well, I put my water right here where it's handy for me, and she reached up on the shelf and took a drink of water. (Laughter) The telephone rang. His mother reached up and took the telephone and answered her call. Johnny didn't even think of yelling into the phone. It took him by surprise. His mother was ready. About noon his mother said, "Well, Johnny, maybe you'd like to have a rest from your learning. Of course, I've got bananas here, and I've got oranges here. I've got sandwiches here. For *my* lunch, if you don't want to take a rest from learning." Johnny said, "I'd like my rest." Mother said, "Well, can we start again at one o'clock?" He started to yell and scream. So she continued sitting there. Johnny took just one lesson.

H: That was a good one.

E: His mother had sandwiches, bananas, oranges, milk, wather, the telephone. A handy book to read. She gave him a rest by letting him roll over on his back. Gave him another rest by letting him roll over on his tummy while she sat on him. He tried to bite her bot-

tom. She said, "Dr. Erickson told me to put on my
tightest girdle and lots and lots of petticoats." Johnny
came in to see me. He said, "Some kids can learn, can't
they." That's right. Some kids can learn. But that
mother was so absolutely desperate.

H: Well, how did you persuade her not to give in at the
crucial point?

E: I pointed out to her that if she gave in at a crucial point,
she was wipped – and the child was whipped. He was
already a neighborhood threat, and a neighborhood
nuisance, and she was going to have to move out of
that neighborhood. The neighbors would not tolerate
it anymore. She had just, about a year before, purchased that new house.

*   *   *

H: You know, the Zen philosophy is that everyone gets
caught up in neurotic patterns, the wheel of life, and
you can suddenly, by dealing with right now, get out
of it. Get out of the pattern. It strikes me that is
similar to your attitude about therapy.

E: Some parents called me a long time ago. Their little girl
was failing in school. In spite of everything on earth
they could do, she was failing. They wanted some
child psychiatry done. They gave me an adequate
description of the little girl, and I went over to see her
in her home. This little girl could not play jacks, and
she could not jump rope, and she could not roller
skate. She could not spell, she could not write, and she
could not read. So I saw her almost every evening.
What did we do? We sat on the floor, and it became
a game – which one of us could be clumsier about playing jacks. It took three weeks before she really started
playing jacks well. Then I spent two weeks on rope
jumping. I could tie a rope to the door knob and swing

it, and she could not jump over it. For that matter, neither could I. It took two weeks for her to learn to jump rope. Then came the matter of the roller skates. So I raised the question of one roller skate. Of course, I can't even use one roller skate. It took her a week to learn to roller skate. She had a bicycle, bought at her request, and for six months she had not tried to ride it. So I arranged with her to come to my office, pushing her bicycle. I said I would race her home. She knew I could ride a bicycle. So we both got on our bicycles, and she was wobbling fearfully. But she saw I was really trying to beat her home. What the little girl did not know was that if I ride a bicycle and really, purposely use my right leg, I cannot pedal fast. If I merely pedal with my left leg, I am an expert at bicycling. But if I use my right leg, it slows up my performance frightfully. She could see that I was honestly trying hard and I really was (laughing). And she beat me home. She had once seen me race her brother on a bicycle, and I used only my left leg, and I had beaten her brother. But *she* beat me. Before the end of the year, she had won the jumping rope contest and the jacks contest, and she came out of school with fine grades. She was elected to the national honor society in high school. She was an all around nice little girl. Now she is married, and she has a child. Not bad for an inadequate, helpless child. Success breeds success. Of course, the little girl could really play jacks, and she could really spell. She could jump rope. And she could accept the fact that she had beat me on the bicycle. I never discussed her relationship with her parents, nor did I give her parents any advice.

H: When you say you don't deal with the little girl on "why," you must have put some thought yourself on why the little girl was the way she was, either in relation to her parents or to something.

E: Well, it was apparent that the girl had lost all confidence in herself. She never measured up to the parental demands. So in a field where the parents could not really be demanding, I let her achieve excellence. With that under her belt . . . (Laughs)

H: Okay.

E: Her parents did not believe in psychiatry. As a last resort, a family doctor advised a psychiatrist. They were humiliated and ashamed at having to ask for psychiatric help. They obviously disapproved of my sitting on the floor and playing jacks. And I can be just as awkward as any incompetent child.

H: Did the parents' disapproval influence the little girl?

E: The fact that they were not quite satisfied with me allowed the little girl to identify with me. I let her discover her own capabilities.

APPENDIX

A Biographical Conversation

*(This conversation took place in 1957 when I was gathering informa-
tion about the life of Milton Erickson for a biographical sketch.)*

Haley: I'd like to know about your parents. Were they born
in this country?

Erickson: My mother is of old New England stock. On her
side of the family, one served in the war of 1812, and
one enlisted and served all through the Civil War.
That's where I got my middle name, Hyland. Major
John Hyland in the war of 1812, originally from Ver-
mont, dating way back to the Pilgrim days. A great-
aunt of mine had a complete genealogy of our entire
family. One day in her dotage she burned it up. Her
statement was simply this: All the descendants should
be able to live on their own merits and not on the past.
So she burned it. I was given my second name when
my mother was 16. This great-aunt was commenting
on the Hylands, how much they had contributed to
this country. She said that no descendant would ever
merit that name. My mother was a 16-year-old girl
then. She said, "When I grow up and get married and
have a baby boy, I'm going to name him Hyland." I
got my first name in another impulsive fashion. I was
born in a mining camp. A neighbor woman from way

down the canyon came up and was holding me, looking at me, and bursting into laughter. Finally, my mother asked curiously, "Why do you laugh everytime you look at the baby?" She said, "I can't help it, he's so homely. What are you naming him?" My mother knew how proud that woman was of her son, and she said, "I'm going to name him Milton after your son."

My father was born in Chicago. His father was an immigrant from Norway. His father died when he was 12. My father went to live with his brother. He was a street urchin, a newsboy, a boot black. He used to wander around Chicago looking at vacant lots, declaring that he planned someday to be a farmer. At 15 he pinned a note to his pillow saying that he had gone to seek his fortune. He went up to Wisconsin. At the age of 16 he saw a farmer driving an old ox cart. He stepped up to the farmer and said, "Don't you want a nice, bright boy on your farm?" The farmer questioned him, and my father gave him a false name: Charley Roberts. Finally, my father talked the old farmer into taking him. So the old farmer on the way home stopped at the farm and said, "You wait here. I have to see my son-in-law." There was a little girl in a red flannel dress playing in the yard. She hid behind a big maple tree. She peeked out coyly from behind the tree, and my father saw her and said, "Whose girl are you?" She coyly answered, "I'm my Daddy's girl." He said, "You're *my* girl now." Seven years later they were married. Three months after the old farmer took "Charley Roberts" into his home, he died suddenly. My father took over the farm, carried my mother's books to school, and fought her battles. Years later, when I was on crutches, I finished out teaching a country school term in the same schoolhouse where my father and mother had gone to school. I was recovering from polio then. After my father married my mother, he went to work in the insane asylum in Juneau, Wisconsin. He worked there for a while, and then he decided to go west to seek his fortune. He'd been there before as a cowboy, went again as a cowboy, a ranger, a miner, a prospector, and finally he and his partner located this rich vein of silver and lead. Had it all developed and well mortgaged, and going to sell it, when the panic broke overnight. So my father was financially ruined. That's why he went east and bought a 10-acre farm.

H: Could we run over a kind of chronology with dates?

E: I was born December 5th, in Aurum, Nevada. It was a mining camp that is now vanished. I was the first child born in Aurum. It was about 10,000 feet above sea level. My father was operating the Silver Bell mine. I was a third child. I left Aurum when I was about three years old in a covered wagon headed east. Then my father bought a small farm in Wisconsin and proceeded to rear a total of nine children on a small farm. One brother six years younger than I, the rest were sisters.

H: What was your mother's name?

E: Clara Minor.

H: And your father?

E: Albert Erickson.

H: Is that their picture on the wall?

E: Yes, on their 62nd wedding anniversary. They've had their 63rd and are looking forward to their 64th.

H: Where are they living now?

E: In Milwaukee. When my father was too old to work the farm, he retired and lived in Milwaukee. Nothing to do after a busy life on the farm, so he hopped on a streetcar and learned how to transfer from one line to another. If there is any street in Milwaukee you want to know, or if you want to know an old-timer keeping a secondhand store, he'll tell you. He knows the entire city. He's got a wealth of interest in everything. My Dad had a wonderful discussion about citrus trees with the old drunk who planted the orange tree in the front yard. That same week the chief justice of the Supreme Court came over to visit him, and my Dad had a wonderful discussion with him on Arizona law, Arizona history, and the development of this state.

H: So you went to school in Wisconsin.

E: I went to grade school in Lowell, Wisconsin and high school in Wishfield, which meant a four-and-a-half-mile walk daily to go to high school. I worked in the summers on a farm, did my share of the farm work. Learned to milk at eight years old. I graduated from high school in 1919 in June. My high school had 30 students in it the year I graduated. My class had six in it. There were two boys. Ed is a professor of Physics at Washington State. Two of my classmates became rural school teachers. One became a switchboard operator and a housewife. The other one became a housewife. The two teachers have since married and become housewives. Economically and socially the entire class was a success. (Laughs) My father and mother only graduated from the 8th grade. Yet because of the endless number of interests they had, and their willingness to learn, they can converse readily with literally anybody.

H: Your mother had that many interests too.

E: Yes, a tremendous number of interests.

H: So you graduated from high school in 1919.

E: Yes, and in August of 1919 I developed infantile paralysis. Finally I began using crutches, and then two canes, and then one cane. By the following summer I had improved enough so that I could take a sitting job in a pea canning factory to earn some money to go to college. The polio hit the right leg and the right arm. With polio, I lost my body sensation very completely. I didn't know where my legs were, and the nurse could put a towel over my face and then put my arm this way, and it was up to me to try to discover, because that was my task, where my arm was. I didn't know whether it was here, or here, or here. I had no idea at all. Then in recovering my body sensations, I might locate my elbow before I located my wrist or my hand or my shoulder. And here would be an elbow floating out in space somewhere out of relationship with the rest of my body. I might locate my thigh but not know where my leg was. I might locate my leg but be unaware of my foot. I might locate my big toe and locate my little toe, on the same foot that is, but have no real relationship. You see with your thumb and your finger – here's the thumb floating in space, and here's the little finger floating in space, but there's no connection such as you ordinarily have. Then I'd spend a good deal of time, morning, afternoon, and evening slowly building up, item by item, that sense of body orientation. Then as I began to recover from the paralysis – how do you move this toe and how do you feel it, and what does your shoulder have to do with a leg movement, because of the tension. Bear this in mind – on knee jerking, tense the hands and the arms and you exaggerate the knee joint.

H: One of the things Gregory Bateson mentioned was that you discussed a speech of President Roosevelt as that of a polio victim. He was talking about how to prepare for the war, and he said we had to do it this way, and this way. You said it was a statement of a polio victim planning to climb some stairs, or planning some physical activity. I wonder how much you think your polio affects this careful and thorough building up you do in hypnosis?

E: I spent hours lying in bed trying to locate, by a sense of feeling, my foot, my toes, because I'd been told that I would be bedridden for the rest of my life. I became acutely aware of what movements were. Then, of course, going into medicine I became aware of what muscles really are. It took me 10 years of time to develop an adequate limp, so that I could limp most efficiently. It made me extremely aware of physical movements, and that came in exceedingly handy in the matter of psychiatry and the matter of hypnosis. Because there are these little telltale movements, these little adjusting movements. You watch a polio victim, the way he tends to measure distances and the feeling of empathy that I have with him. That's one reason that I could recognize the gait of any of my fellow employees at the hospital. Because so much of our communication is on bodily movements, not just speech. The fact that I'm tone deaf makes me pay attention to inflections and not to be distracted by the content. My ability to recognize a good piano player, not by the noise he makes but by the ways his fingers touch the keys. That sure touch, delicate touch, a forceful touch, but it's so accurate. It's such a nice physical movement.

H: What you seem to have done is get the most out of a handicap.

E: Is it a handicap or an asset?

H: Yes. (Laughs) Something in the way you often approach a task somehow rang a bell for me in the way Gregory was describing what you said about Roosevelt. I'm wondering if you would know whether that kind of an approach existed prior or after the polio?

E: For me? It would be pretty hard for me to tell.

H: It's a maximum anticipation of what's going to happen, or what comes next.

E: Yet, in a way, I did show some understanding. As a little kid I watched the farmers pitching hay, and they would complain about their aching shoulders. I asked them why they didn't pitch hay right and left handedly, to hoe right and left handedly, to use an axe right and left handedly, and to do it with equal skill merely as a matter of doing it more equally. A maximum number of approaches to the matter.

H: After your first polio attack, you must have been in pretty good shape if you could work in a pea canning factory.

H: Not too good shape. But I also worked building highways, shoveling sand and gravel. The shoveling sand and gravel was out of a boxcar, and I would brace myself against the side of the car, or kneel down, and shovel that way. By using a rhythmical pattern of shoveling, I didn't tire myself too much and I could produce.

After my first year of college, I was called in by the health department at the university and informed that I had to get a great deal of exercise, and be out in the open and not use my legs. So that first summer, after that first year at college, I went on a canoe trip that lasted from June 14 to September. I went through the lakes of Madison and down the O'hare River, down the Rock River, down the Mississippi River to a few miles above St. Louis, then turned back and went up the Illinois River, then through the Hennipen canal, back to the Rock River, up to the O'hare River and back to Madison. I covered about 1200 miles in the canoe. I started out with 2 dollars and 32 cents capital to live on for that summer. I wore a knotted handkerchief on my head, and a swimming suit. I did have a shirt and a pair of overalls and a pair of sneakers. Most of the time I was in the swimming suit and wearing that knotted handkerchief. I started out in the 17-foot canoe with a small bag of beans and a small bag of rice. Tin pails, a canteen, and a skillet.

A knife and fork, and a hatchet, and two blankets. I picked up my living along the river, fishing, wild plants. There are a lot of edible plants that grow along the river bank.

When I hit the Mississippi river, I was in clover because the steamers there peeled potatoes by the bushel basket. They dumped the peelings out, and there are always a few potatoes lost in the peelings, and they float. The same with apples. Now and then a banana would be floating, or some tomatoes. I always harvested them. Another thing, I could also paddle within hailing distance of a fishing boat. Since I wore that knotted handkerchief and I tan very deeply, a fisherman was always curious and would hail me and ask me a few questions. I'd tell him I was a pre-med student at the University of Wisconsin canoeing for my health. They wanted to know how the fishing was, and I would tell them the day was yet young. They invariably gave me fish without my asking. Usually they tried to give me a catfish, I always refused it. Catfish were much more expensive, and they made their living fishing. So they would give me about double or three times the amount of Mississippi perch.

Another thing, along the river there's always picnic grounds. You set up your camp there, because picnic parties always bring much more food than they can eat. And I'd cook up a pail full of oatmeal, or rice or beans. The picnic party would come over and look at it scornfully. I always inherited the extra food they didn't want to take home. Now and then camping along the river I'd get a chance to work. One man was cleaning up some secondhand brick, building a sorghum mill. So he suggested that instead of camping in his pasture, why didn't I come up and sit down on a box and clean brick. He said, I'll pay you so much an hour, and you can sleep in a bed. So I got three days' work and a bed, and all I could eat, and I got paid for it! After that, at another place, I watched cows while they were building a fence. It's all I had to do was watch cows and milk them at night and the next morning, 16 cows. I got a bed and 50 cents a day. In that way I earned enough money to buy myself a pup tent, and some oatmeal and some cornmeal.

Then one place on the Rock River, I was sitting at the camp one night near the river shore, and a great big truck came along with two rough-looking, bearded men. They stopped the truck and said, "What are you doing here, kid?" I said, "I'm setting up camp." They promptly told me there was no place to camp. I told them I was going to camp. They told me they wouldn't let me. I swung my hatchet and asked them why they thought I couldn't camp within 30 feet of a navigable river? They said, "No crippled kid like you is going to camp out like that. We live on an island up the stream about a half mile. We got a bed there for you, and that's where you're going to camp." So I went up there and they turned out to be a couple of hoodlums with hearts of gold. They hauled my canoe out of the water, fixed it up, practically carried me up and put me in a rocking chair. They baked some biscuits and fried some meat for me, furnished a bed for me, and insisted I stay there all summer. Their history? They camped out during the summer. Marv fished for clam shells. Pete bought cattle. When winter came, since they had no home and couldn't live on the island, they usually went into Rockford, Illinois with a brick. They smashed a plate glass window and got sentenced to 90 days at the house of correction.

I stayed there two weeks, being well fed and getting in some swimming and some paddling around. Then I moved on down the river. They were disappointed to see me go but made me promise to stop in and see them if I came back.

When I started out I couldn't pull my canoe out of water. I could swim about 25 feet. I didn't have a pup tent. I just camped wherever I could. By the time I got back, my chest measurement had increased six inches. I could paddle upstream 50 miles in a day, from 6 in the morning until 10 at night—50 miles upstream against a four-mile current. I had a tremendous shoulder and chest development. I could swing up my canoe over my head and carry it up a dam. And going downstream, when I came to a dam, there were always posts around them. I'd shinny up a post and sit there in my trunks and my knotted handkerchief on my head reading a German book that I took along. People would gather at that sight. I'd always tell them I was waiting to get my canoe over the dam. It was always volunteer service. (Laughter)

H: You had decided early to go to medical school?

E: In deciding to be a doctor, I once suffered—at the age of eight—a very severe toothache. I went to the family doctor who not only pulled that tooth and eased the pain, but gave me a great big nickel, thereby making me the richest man in the world and the happiest. Right then and there I swore that when I grew up I'd be a doctor and make people happy. Thereafter I adhered to that idea of being a doctor.

H: When did you develop the interest in hypnosis?

E: At the age of 12, one of the local boys sent away for a cheap pamphlet on hypnosis. He wanted to hypnotize me. I told him I was going to wait until I was a man and knew something, and I'd learn hypnosis and really learn it. I didn't learn anything about hypnosis until at the close of my second year in college. I witnessed Clark L. Hull demonstrate for the pre-medics. I took one of the subjects to my room and worked on him. I hypnotized another student, and then another stu-

dent. That summer I started hypnotizing my sisters,
my brother, and some of the kids in Lowell, Wisconsin. Every spare bit of time I had spent hypnotizing,
devising various techniques and various ways of getting hypnotic subjects to do things. When I got back
for my third year of college, Hull established a seminar on hypnosis. I reported in full on all the work I
had done in my spare time during the summer. Hull
and the graduate students in psychology discussed
the meaning of it. Also during that year I did a lot
of experimental work with college students as hypnotic subjects, and I would report on that each week
at the seminar. With the result, by the end of my third
year in college I had hypnotized several hundred people and carried on quite a number of experiments in
the laboratory. I also demonstrated hypnosis at the
Mendota State Hospital, and for various professors
in the medical school and the psychology department.

H: What year did you graduate from medical school?

E: 1928. Getting a job was difficult. I had to take part-time
my first year in medical school, and I worked with the
state board of control. I majored in psychology as a
pre-medical student, and Professor Clarke Powell had
recommended me to the State Board of Control where
Frank Richmond headed the psychiatric field department. So I did psychological examinations in the prison system in Wisconsin, including Milwaukee, and the
orphanages.

H: Giving examinations to the prisoners?

E: Yes, to all the inmates. Boys' industrial school, girls'
industrial school, Milwaukee County House of Cor-
rections, the women's reformatory, the young men's
reformatory, the women's state prison, and the men's
state prison. The state prison for the criminally insane. The state home for neglected and dependent
children. And then various jails and orphanages.

H: This was while you were going to medical school, or after?

E: While I was going. So I actually enrolled in medical school for five years. Getting through the first year, when I wanted to be full-time in medical school, there was one serious difficulty—no job. So I went down to the State Board of Control, and beginning in September, every week I had one or two statistical reports on criminality put on the desk of the President of the State Board of Control. They were things he was interested in for getting better appropriations, getting news story releases. Then in November, the first Monday, there was no report. The president was furious, and he demanded that I be called in. He asked me point blank what I was being paid for. Why didn't I have more reports? I told him I wasn't being paid anything. So he said, "Well, if that's the case you're on the payroll right now!" So that settled my job. In addition to that on every holiday, or vacation, I was paid my expenses and a per diem for some special examination the state board wanted. So I was steadily involved. Christmas vacation, if I remember correctly, I was paid 10 dollars a day plus expenses to do examinations. So I managed to make enough money. Also, my first year in medical school I arrived with $75. I bicycled around Madison looking for some opportunity. I saw a house for rent at $70 per month. I looked it over, saw the landlord, gave him $70, and put up a sign, "Rooms for Students." I talked the registrar into delaying the payment of fees. I took in students who were working their way through and were delighted to furnish their own linens at a reduced rent. I talked some secondhand storage companies into letting me store some beds and some furniture for them. So I had the place furnished, and the rooms rented out. That essentially paid my way through medical school. Plus the regular salary from the Board of Control. I really had a very nice time.

H: Were you planning then to go into psychiatry?

E: In high school they taught a course in psychology, and I looked through the book and decided to wait until I got to the university before I studied psychology. It was too important a subject to try to study in high school. So when I got to the university, I started in on psychology. That, of course, crystalized my interest in psychiatry. And throughout medical school I knew I was going into psychiatry. I interned in Colorado, a special internship at Colorado Psychopathic Hospital of three months' duration. While looking for a placement, I did some special research work on child psychiatry, analyzing the case histories of about 1200 children. I summarized it, got a job in Rhode Island as Senior Psychiatrist, writing my thesis for my Bachelor's degree. I had postponed that, because I wanted to write a thesis that would be interesting rather than routine. In my State Board of Control work, examining all the convicts gave me an opportunity to make a study of crime in various relationships. So I wrote a thesis on that. Murchison had done a study on intelligence and crime, and I did another. Then I also wrote on feeble-mindedness, abandonment, and crime. When I presented my Bachelor's thesis, the committee looked it over and offered me my choice. I had enrolled in graduate school anyway, and the committee told me "we can give you an honors on your thesis, or we'll accept it as a combined Master's and Bachelor's thesis." So I preferred to take the combined thesis rather than honors, because that gave me my Master's degree.

H: When you say you delayed the Bachelor's, was it in medical school that you finished it?

E: While I was in medical school.

H: You mean you got your Master's along the way while you were getting your medical degree.

E: Yes. While I was in medical school, I lacked some credits for my Master's degree. Mathematics, for one thing, trigonometry. So I went to the head of the department of mathematics and explained I had physiology at the same hour trigonometry was given. Would he let me skip the trigonometry class if I could guarantee to get a passing grade of 90. If it were 89, I'd take a flunk. He was an awfully nice man, and he said that it was against the university rules to permit cuts, but if I wanted to take that chance I could. So I took make-up exams, and I came out with a grade of 90. I took my Latin the same way. I wanted to take some other courses, and I had been studying while driving on the milk route, during high school and during the summer. I purchased a Latin textbook and studied Latin throughout the summer for two summers, because Latin was not taught in the high school I went to. So when I got to college, I asked permission from the Latin department to enroll in the Latin class but just skip it. I guaranteed a grade of 93. I actually got a grade of 97. I took some German courses the same way. I didn't want to waste time in German class, and I knew the habit of the professor who taught the class. When she was through teaching that hour, she always went to the German library. There she would find me reading a German novel much more advanced than was being given in German. It was a very difficult way of learning German, but I had another class at the German hour. I proved by my ability to read German novels that it would be all right for me to skip beginning German. One year in medical school, I carried 31 hours one semester and the next one I started to carry 33 hours because there were a lot of additional courses I wanted to take. I didn't get hourly credit for them, I only got course credit in case I wanted a Ph.D. also.

I paid for my room the first year in medical school by the simple process of rooming in a rooming house where the landlady was 70 years old. I did her cooking and her baking and her shopping and attended her furnace. That way I got plenty of good food, and all I wanted to eat.

That publication of my combined Master's and Bachelor's thesis was very helpful when I applied for a job at the Rhode Island State Hospital. Noyes, past president of the American Psychiatric Association, was very much interested in someone who had just completed his internship and who had already published — some three papers I think it was I had published. So he hired me as senior on the service. When I arrived there he outlined my duties and asked if I knew of anybody who wanted a junior position. So I looked over the junior position, and instead of taking $2,500 a year in the senior position, I took the $1,960 job and a junior position. First thing I did, I was assigned the reception service, and I started doing extensive mental examinations, and psychometric examinations. Then there was a special project; to get acquainted with psychiatric patients as quickly as possible, I started doing mental examinations on all the patients in the reception building, which made a very good impression on Dr. Noyes.

There was an opening on the research service at Worchester State Hospital, and he recommended me for that position. I had heard about Worchester State Hospital when I was at Colorado. I was informed that anybody who ever wanted to learn something in psychiatry ought to spend some time there, because every well-known psychiatrist in the United States had been at Worchester State Hospital at least some time. Adolf

Meyer started there, Brill was there, and so on. When Dr. Noyes recommended that I go there, I very gladly took the job there as junior psychiatrist in the research service. Soon I was senior psychiatrist and then was made chief psychiatrist.

I had not been allowed to do any work in hypnosis during my internship at Colorado General. I didn't dare mention it. They had investigated me when I applied for the internship, to make certain I was a respectable medical student. I was warned that I would lose my internship if I did any hypnosis. All through medical school I had been doing hypnotic work. The department of pharmacology had sponsored me, Clark Hull had sponsored me. The dean of the medical school had sponsored me, and the Department of Internal Medicine had favored it. So I had been well protected in medical school. When it came to the question of internship, there was a lot of doubt because there had been some newspaper publicity. When I got to Rhode Island, Dr. Noyes warned me that the Board of Supervisors would not tolerate any hypnosis. So that had to be abandoned. But when I got to Worchester on the research service, separate from the main hospital, the general attitude was, "anything goes." From chiropractic to hypnosis. So I published a number of papers there and did a great deal of experimental work.

The Wayne County General Hospital, Eloise, Michigan, had been looking for several years for someone to head the department of psychiatric research and training. There was a staff of seven men and over 3,000 patients, psychiatric patients. None of the staff was well trained in psychiatry. So they hired me as the director of psychiatric research and training at a considerably greater salary than I was receiving at Worchester and a considerably greater salary than the men on the staff had. The statement to me was, "You are window dressing. I want to force the Board

of Supervisors to improve this staff. With you here
at a high salary, I can argue now that we've got to
have a staff in keeping with you." The result was that
he was able to enforce his plan. The staff jumped from
seven men to 26 men, and the salaries went up all
around. I went to Eloise in 1934 in the spring, and I
met the Professor of Psychiatry at the Wayne University College of Medicine. We discussed psychiatry,
and he promptly asked me to substitute for him because he felt he was getting old. So I started in as an
Instructor, and he promptly promoted me to Assistant Professor. Then I got certified in psychiatry, so
I was made Associate Professor in 1939. I had been
working in association with the Psychology Department instructing students, training psychology students in clinical psychology. Every summer I had one
or two interns in clinical psychology. I supervised a
Master's thesis, a Ph.D. thesis, for the psychology department, both at Wayne University and at the University of Michigan. I also taught in the Social Service Department with the result that Wayne University
named me full Professor in the graduate school. As
a result of my hypnotic work, Michigan State College
offered me a Professorship in Clinical Psychology. So
I taught there in addition.

H: In addition? All these simultaneously?

E: Yes. With the development of the war, I also worked
at the Induction Board. I worked in the wards substituting, so I could combine my Board work with the
teaching of medical students. I'd take the medical
students there and give them a course in applied,
clinical psychiatry, discussing the inductees with them
as they went through. The medical students were very
appreciative. I also took down students in clinical
psychology, so that they could have some actual clinical experience.

H: Just what was "Eloise"?

E: Eloise was established over 100 years ago as the Wayne County Poor Farm. They brought out a psychotic person, and then they tended to bring out more. Finally they had enough patients there so they needed a Post Office. The Superintendent was asked to supply a name. He said he had list after list of names for the post office. Finally, as a joke, he added his granddaughter's name, Eloise. That was the one the Post Office accepted. At the time I was there, Eloise had about 4,000 – over 3,000 when I arrived, and 4,000 by the time I left – mentally ill patients in a 1,500 bed general hospital. And 3,000 to 5,000 poor farm inmates, all under one general superintendency. So the population ranged continuously from 7,000 to 11,000. You had every conceivable kind of psychosis and physical disorder imaginable. As a research place, I had all the material you could ever imagine. Students of anthropology would come in there and spend a few weeks.

H: Was it officially a state hospital?

E: No, it's a county hospital. Then in the 1940s it was decided to change the name from the Eloise Hospital and Infirmary to the Wayne County General Hospital and Infirmary. Because it was county property. The Post Office still remained Eloise, Michigan. The entire town of Eloise is the hospital.

H: Did you live on the hospital grounds?

E: We lived on the hospital grounds, just as we had at Worchester, Massachusetts. Rhode Island also. Then in 1947, I rode a bike, because walking was hard. I fell off the bike, and I got a very nasty gash in my forehead. A lot of dirt got thoroughly ground into it. I knew I was sensitive to horse serum, and I had not taken any anti-tetanus toxin. So I spent a couple of days deciding whether I should take the risk of the anti-tetanus serum or not. All the medical advice was,

"You'll have to risk it." So I took it, and seven days later I developed anaphylactic shock which required repeated emergency treatment with adrenalin. For the next 15 months I was up and down with serum sickness. Joint pains, muscle pains, and sudden collapse from the serum sickness. The result was that I became increasingly sensitive to pollen. I'd always suffered from hay fever, and my sensitivity to pollens increased tremendously, with the result that I landed in the hospital several times in rather serious condition. I was advised to leave Michigan and seek another climate entirely. I studied the map, and that led to the selection of Phoenix, Arizona. I came here in July, 1948. I spent the summer regaining my health and then joined a friend of mine at the Arizona State Hospital. He was the superintendent. I had known him in Detroit, Michigan. The Arizona State Hospital was badly understaffed. So we started planning to build up the hospital. During the course of the six months I was there, I received letters from various medical schools from students asking if they could take their psychiatric residency here. But the Arizona State Hospital up to that time had been famous for the political brawls that resulted in changes in administration. I had been there from October until April when the superintendent resigned and I resigned and a couple of others. I went into private practice here. It was my intention to stay at the Arizona State Hospital for about a year and work to build it up and then go into private practice. I went into practice six months earlier, as it was. I left Michigan on July 1, arrived here on a leave of absence with pay. That was continued until I notified them that I was resigning. I resigned, I think it was October 14, from Eloise and assumed my duties at Arizona State Hospital that same day. I joined it as a staff physician and very soon was the Clinical Director and Acting Assistant Superintendent.

H: Was this the first time you had gone into private practice?

E: Even in Worchester, Massachusetts, I was not supposed to have private patients. I accepted private patients, and it was condoned because I did not charge them. Instead, in return for psychiatric help, they served as experimental cases, or they gave permission to use the data for publication. So it was esentially a research proposition. When I went to Michigan, I was not supposed to accept private patients, but it was finally agreed that I could. Some for pay and some for experimental investigation and exploratory purposes. At Michigan, as a result of my publications and a lot of newspaper publicity my writings got, there were a tremendous number of people who came out there to see me. I could select interesting cases. Being Director of Psychiatric Research and Training, I always had my choice of the patients in the hospital.

I would do a very careful mental examination of a new patient and avoid getting any historical material at all. Just get his delusional content, his hallucinatory content, and a good description of his affective reactions. From that material I would go and write a social service history of him. The other thing was to read the social service history on a patient, and then write, from speculation, the mental examination on the patient. I did that extensively in order to compare my speculations with the actuality. The result was that it helped me to judge better all the time what really to expect from this hallucination or this delusion, or what to expect from this experiential thing. I did that for four years at Worchester.

H: What did you include in a mental examination?

E: General behavior and attitude. Then the structure of

the language, and the ideational content. Now of course you get some historical data, but you would not necessarily get anything about the father, the mother, the brother or the sisters, the uncle, the aunts. Insight and judgment. The character of the affect.

H: You were married when?

E: I married the first time in 1925. I was very idealistic. "I'm married and I'm going to be happy." I soon found out if I had any happiness it would be in the children. Bert, Lance, and Carol came along. There was a divorce, and to hell with idealistic ideas about marriage. Then I saw a pretty girl walking across campus at the University of Michigan in March. I decided I would marry that girl. In August, I got my divorce. The next week I dated that girl and got engaged to her.

H: She became an assistant of yours?

E: Yes, I did not know her name. I called up Wayne University and said I wanted an assistant to work with me in some research. They sent that girl I had seen on the campus of the University of Michigan. She was attending the Academy of Arts there. So I hired her as an assistant on June 18. My divorce did not clear until August. As soon as I got my divorce, I dated her. Then she finished college. It was on June 18th that I got my Bachelor's degree, my M.A. degree, and my M.D. degree. I hired Betty as my assistant on June 18. She graduated on June 18 and we were married on June 18. Allan was an induced labor so he would not arrive on June 18 and would have a birthday all his own.

H: I take it that none of your children, like Bert and Lance, have shown any particular interest either in hypnosis or medical school.

E: No. Both Bert and Lance said that a doctor works too hard. Because I did work hard. I spent my evenings doing research, studying, reading. Even though I did play with them. I used to tell the children "White Tummy" stories about a froggy with a green back and a white tummy. I've taken "White Tummy" through thousands and thousands of adventures. With Bert, Lance, Carol, Betty Alice, Allan, Bobby, Roxy, and Kristy.* Since I'm color blind in large part, and purple is one color I see, I use that.

H: Is your colorblindness around reds?

E: Red and green.

H: I take it you never had analysis as part of training.

E: I've consulted various analysts, some of the leading analysts in the country, discussing this possibility. There statement to me was, "Why don't you follow your own field of interest? You'll probably contribute more that way."

H: I notice even in your early paper, "Ejaculatio Praecox," in 1934, you were pretty psychoanalytic about it.

E: I've always been interested in psychoanalysis. I've read extensively, but better than that I've discussed it with quite a few psychoanalysts.

H: Were you ever a good subject for hypnosis?

E: I learned about hypnosis by myself without reading any books, just trying it. I taught a lot of people. But they were all my students. As the years went by, I'm still in contact with my students. I've tried repeatedly to go into trance for somebody. I can do auto hypnosis, but I never developed a heterohypnotic trance.

H: I believe you mentioned at the seminar that you use auto hypnosis for pain.

E: For pain? That's right. And to write papers. Not the entire paper, to check over what I have written. For ex-

---

*The Erickson children are as follows: Albert, born in 1929; Lance, born in 1931; Carol, born in 1934; Betty Alice, born in 1938; Allan, born in 1941; Bobby, born in 1945; Roxy, born in 1949. Kristina, born in 1951, was the only child to become a physician.

ample, one paper I had written, and I had written it from memory rather than the case record. That night when I went to bed, I was thinking, "Tomorrow I'll get out the record and compare my written account with the actual case record." That night, as I often do, I had a dream. I was back in Michigan. I worked with my patient there. I had all the data laid out, and I really went through every bit of it. Examining it to see what parts I would use when I wrote the paper. The next day I got out the case record; I had really reviewed it completely.

H: And you consider that dream "auto hypnosis"?

E: Yes, because when I go to sleep I intend to have a dream in which I'll cover something. I never know exactly what it is that I will cover. Then maybe I'll have a dream and not know it for a week. Then all of a sudden an idea will come to me that I better write this. I don't know what I'm going to write until I've finished writing it, and then the dreams will come to me. I dreamed it through, and maybe a week later recorded it.

H: You can deliberately set out to have a dream and have it?

E: Yes, but not necessarily remember it the next morning. Sometimes I'll go three weeks, or a month. I'll mislay a manuscript unconsciously. I know better than to try and find it. Maybe a month later, I find it accidentally. What happens that day? A special patient that I want to include in that paper comes in that day. Of course, I'd known a month ago that the patient was coming in a month. Here I discover my manuscript is very fresh in my mind, see my patient, and recognize why and how I should use the data from that patient.

H: When you do auto hypnosis, is it this kind of thing, like producing a dream, or do you manage to go into a trance on your own?

E: I can sit here at my desk and interview a patient and feel that I can understand the patient better if I were in an auto hypnotic trance. I go into an auto hypnotic trance, and deal with the patient adequately enough so the patient returns. I dismiss the patient and then come out of the hypnotic trance, look at the clock, and realize that I must have completed the interview. What are my notes? There are none, so I pick up my pen, and one by one the notes come.

H: You mean when you wake up you have amnesia for the interview?

E: I have amnesia for the interview. I merely pick up my pen and start writing. The first note. So I make a conscious note of that, and I write it down and read it. It's a very delightful experience.

H: (Laughs) Is this amnesia inevitable from your auto hypnosis?

E: Not always.

H: If you always went that deep it would be?

E: A Professor of Psychiatry was my patient and suddenly discovered that I was in a deep auto hypnotic trance. He got very alarmed. He started yelling at me to awaken. (Laughter) I tried to explain to him I was in an auto hypnotic trance, but that didn't satisfy him. So I had to interrupt my trance and wake up. I explained my use of it to him, that I could understand him better at an unconscious level. He's about the only patient that ever recognized the auto hypnotic trance.

H: Was he a hypnotist himself?

E: He had experience with hypnosis.

H: Have you ever used time distortion yourself?

E: I have unintentionally, accidentally.

H: I could use some of that to help organize this interview.

E: My second attack of polio was in 1953. I lost a whole lot more muscles in my arm, my back, my sides, my abdomen, the right leg, and the left leg. I was once able to chin myself three times with my right arm, four or five with my left. I could chin myself 25 times in succession with both arms, especially after my canoe trip. But now it is difficult to just get my arm up. I'm a lot more unsteady on my feet since 1953.

H: This was another strain of polio?

E: Yes.

H: So you have had two of the three strains?

E: One more to go.

H: That's remarkable. Have you ever heard of people getting them both?

E: Oh yes. There's a girl over in Mesa. I think there have been several reported in the literature. I'm still learning new movements with my arm and with my leg.

H: I notice when you smoke a cigarette, you keep it in your right hand. Is that to keep it in use?

E: Yes. I don't have an extension phone in here for a very deliberate reason. To walk from here to the telephone repeatedly gives me a certain amount of necessary exercise. Or else I'd be sitting here too long. Yet a year ago Easter, in spite of the second attack of polio, I made one of the difficult mountain climbs. With two canes.

H: You seem much improved from how you were at the seminar in March of last year, so I gather the more you use the muscles the better.

E: I was having a tremendous amount of pain in my muscles at that seminar. Just an immense, horrible amount of pain. At the present time I had to triple my intake of calcium to prevent muscle cramps. I can get muscle cramps that are so severe that they tear the muscles. Not long ago I got a cramp in this muscle here, and it caused an inter-muscular hemorrhage. That really hurt!

H: Can you influence the pain with an auto hypnotic trance?

E: Often, if the cramp starts slowly enough, but when it comes like that, it's there, and all you can think of – well, you can't really think. I've lost the muscles in my mouth, my tongue. Perhaps you've noticed now and then my speech slurs? Have you noticed my facial paralysis? It shows up beautifully on photographs. The right side is partially paralyzed.

H: I noticed when you were imitating anger you were using both sides of your face.

E: It's not extended. But like wiggling your ears, I don't know how. I had even wrestled in college. Because my movements were so very, very quick. I could substitute quickness of movement for power of movement. I did a lot of wrestling – not in a gym, in a house. One of my favorite sports.

H: Getting back to your work, one of the things that has puzzled me a bit is where you--do you particularly get a unique kind of patient? I mean you get more odd patients than anyone I know. It might be because you write them up that it's interesting, or it might be they just come to you. I never heard of problems like having to pee through a tube and that sort of thing.

E: Good heavens, I even encountered them when I was a kid on the farm. The average psychiatrist does not ever try to find out those things. What's odd and peculiar about you? What is the thing that you'd least like to tell me? And it's perfectly amazing the things that I hear.

H: I just wondered if those people seek out a hypnotist.

E: Yes, there's a tendency for that. They consider themselves so odd and so peculiar they seek out another odd one. (Laughs) Patients seem to run in cycles. I hadn't had an alcoholic for a year; the same week I got two beautiful alcoholics. Both pathological intoxications. That is, they drank infrequently but as soon as they drank they were berserk, and I mean berserk.

Two in one week, and the pathological intoxication is relatively rare. I suppose it would be interesting to set down the patients in order of diagnosis. At the induction board we didn't see a single multiple sclerosis for one whole year, and then one day we saw six of them.

H: I gather from your papers that you did a lot of quick therapy with some of the men being inducted, to help them get in.

E: I don't know how many draft boards I was a consultant for around Detroit. There were special cases, borderline cases; I saw a tremendous number. Peculiar material.

H: Your papers show it.

E: I think you can write up a dozen or two dozen routine schizophrenics and you haven't contributed any more than the other fellow who has written up a dozen routine schizophrenics. But if you run across one case that illustrates some point uniquely and clearly and understandably, then you've actually contributed. How many appendectomies are written up each year? They used a different kind of catgut. In teaching, all the students always sent their odd friends to me. Of course, there's a certain prestige that somebody known to hypnotize has, so it attracts people.

H: One of the things Gregory Bateson has said, and I'm never sure what Gregory says about you, how much of it is fantasy and how much isn't, because he feels there's a magical quality in all this. He said that once when you were giving a lecture, there was a man in the audience who disagreed with you. You knew about it beforehand. While you were giving a lecture on a scientific subject you induced that man to agree with you.

E: Yes.

H: Can you tell me about that?

E: The man is now a Professor of Psychology at Harvard University. His theory of hypnosis was that the subject behaves as the operator defines. And Fremont-Smith organized a seminar, something on emotions, and I knew this man was there and that he disagreed with me about hypnosis. I disagreed emphatically with *his* theory. During the course of that lecture, which had been prepared ahead of time – I didn't know that the man was going to be there – it finally wound up with the man agreeing not only with my lecture but agreeing that I was right in discrediting his book.

H: Well, now how did you manage this? What was the lecture on?

E: Damned if I remember now.

H: Did you do it by an emphasis on certain words?

E: An emphasis on certain words. And in looking around at the group, fixing my eye on him.

H: You didn't induce a trance in him?

E: Well, he was a bit afraid of me. I carefully directed a word, or a phrase, or a clause at him. Margaret Mead thought that he went into a trance. Bateson thought that he went into a trance. Bateson and Mead were very impressed with what I did to that man.

H: It impressed Gregory, I know that. It has made him very uneasy. (Laughs)

E: Well, of course the man had to be shaky in his own beliefs to do that. Somewhere in my files I have a letter from him written since I've been in Phoenix, praising me very highly and again expressing doubts about his theory. It was written in conjunction with sending one of his prize students to spend the summer with me.

INDEX